A MANAGER'S GUIDE TO

OPERATIONS RESEARCH

A Manager's Guide to Operations Research

RUSSELL L. ACKOFF

Past President, Operations Research Society of America
Professor of Operations Research, Case Institute of Technology
Cleveland, Ohio

PATRICK RIVETT

Professor of Operational Research, University of Lancaster, England
Past President, Operational Research Society, United Kingdom

1963
JOHN WILEY & SONS
New York · London · Sydney

To

CLAY H. HOLLISTER

and

DONALD HICKS

The Managers who guided Us

Preface

OVER THE last twenty years the science of OR has grown rapidly. It has grown not only in the sophistication of the techniques which it uses, not only in the rapid intake of the personnel employed, not only in the rapid increase of the salaries of all those working in this field, but it has also grown in the type of problem it tackles and in the maturity it brings to these problems. Such has been its rapid growth that notwithstanding the great deal of interaction between the OR scientist and the industrialist, the management executive often hasn't a clue what it is that the OR men in his company are doing. For the man who does not yet have OR within his company, there is the perplexing problem of whether he should undertake OR and, if he does, what is going to happen, what sort of people will he employ and how will they go about their business. To introduce OR into a company requires a tremendous act of faith on the part of the executive.

Justification by faith is a well established doctrine, but equally faith without understanding is a questionable basis for managerial action. It is the purpose of this book to enable the industrial executive to reduce the faith he requires to undertake OR in his organization. The techniques of OR are now so highly developed that it is difficult, and in fact probably not very useful, to take the executive through them. In fact, one wonders how far the industrial executive needs to know the manipulative techniques of his staff. Should the executives of a chemical company be able to analyze a compound for the presence of copper? Should the executives of a petroleum company be able to operate an oil refinery? We feel the answer here is, No. What we do feel, however, is that there is a need for the executive to become acquainted with what OR is doing, with how the OR worker goes about his task and what is likely to be involved in setting up OR.

Over the last 15 years we have both, in our own and each other's countries, met hundreds of executives who have come up with the same pattern of questions regarding the use of OR. In comparing our notes while writing this book, we have been fascinated to find how common is our experience in this regard. It seemed to us that we would like to share the answers to these questions so that the industrial executive may be able to find out a little bit about this field for himself and may be introduced to some of the introductory references for reading in this area. Equally, we hope that this book will appeal to the harassed OR worker who is called upon within his company, from time to time, if not from week to week, to explain what it is he is doing and how he goes about it and how he fits in with the whole picture of industrial OR. It is, therefore, at the industrial executive that we have aimed this book, in the hope that it will be of assistance and encouragement to him.

We should like to express our appreciation to Frank Benson, Glen D. Camp and Vern Mickelson for their helpful suggestions in preparing this work.

Patrick Rivett
Russell L. Ackoff

Contents

1 The Nature of OR

The evolution of management and related scientific aids

Let us begin this story with a familiar part of our past. Until the second half of the last century, most industrial organizations in the United States and United Kingdom employed only a handful of people and occupied a space about the size of a two-car garage. These enterprises were usually owned and managed by the same individual.

This picture began to change in the last quarter of the nineteenth century because of the first industrial revolution. This revolution was based on the development of power-generating equipment and machine tools. Mechanization of production, together with the development of national transportation and establishments with an eye to the sources of material and labor and to the location of consumers, rather than to natural sources of power. As industrial enterprises expanded, it was no longer possible for one man to perform all the necessary managerial functions. Consequently mechanization, which led to a division of manual labor, also led to a division of managerial labor. Functional managers were created, usually responsible for production, marketing, finance, personnel, and engineering or research and development.

Industries continued to grow and required further division of managerial functions. For example, a new level of production management was sometimes created to care for such functions as shop operations, maintenance, procurement, quality control, and transportation. As companies merged or expanded into multi-plant operations, this complex of managers then had to be reproduced in several locations. That is, product diversification and the geographical expansion of the market required still further segmentation of management. This process of segmentation continues even now.

Throughout this division of management and the growth of industry, the scientists, whose research had helped to make it possible, turned to the new class of problems created by the application of the instruments and knowledge that they had produced. Some physical scientists became experts in power, machines, and materials and began to differentiate themselves from other physical scientists on the basis of their interests in industry and their preoccupation with the application of available knowledge rather than with the discovery of new knowledge. In this way mechanical engineering came into existence as a development of applied physics. Chemists and engineers together created chemical engineering. For a quarter of a century or more, mechanical and chemical engineers concentrated on increasing the productivity of the equipment employed in the productive process.

In the early part of the twentieth century, it became apparent that further significant increases in productivity could only be obtained by giving more attention to the worker than he had hitherto received. Taking advantage of the newly developing science of psychology, a number of engineers began to study the interactions of man and the machine which he operated. In this way, industrial engineering and work study were born.

Similar applications of science were made to other functions of business. For the marketing function, statistics, economics, psychology, and sociology were combined to create market and marketing research. In finance, the economics of the firm (or micro-economics) was created, and accounting grew into a profession. In the human area, industrial psychology and sociology developed out of the study of human relations in industry. Science kept pace with the specialization of management. For example, in production, statistical quality control and engineering specialities in maintenance, procurement, transportation and materials handling, all came into existence.

In this parallel development of management and applied science, however, there was one conspicuous gap. Except for a few abortive efforts, science did not come to the aid of the *executive* function created by the segmentation of management. Before we examine this and the reasons for it, let us consider the nature of the executive function.

The function of an executive consists, among other things, of integrating the policies and operations of the diverse departments reporting to him, in order to obtain an overall operation that comes as close as possible to realizing the organization's overall objectives. This integrating function is quite complex because of the conflict of interests that always develop between the units coordinated by an executive.

For example, in a functional type of organization, the executive wants to evaluate separately the performance of each function. To do so, objectives are established for each function. The objective of the production department is usually formulated as 'to maximize output and to minimize the unit production costs'. For marketing, the objective might be 'to maximize sales volume and to minimize the unit cost of sales'. For finance it might be 'to minimize the capital required to operate the business'. For personnel, it might be 'to maximize employee morale' or, more specifically, 'to minimize labor turnover'.

Like the ten commandments, these objectives represent aspirations which are easier to accept in principle than to follow in practice. Practical difficulty arises out of their inconsistency. Consider, for example, the question of an appropriate inventory policy for the company.

Each function has a different concept of what inventory policy should be because of the difference in objectives. The production department would like to make long continuous manufacturing runs in order to minimize setups and in order to get the efficiency that comes with long practice. To produce in this way requires a large inventory spread over relatively few products. Therefore, from the production department's point of view, the shorter the product line, the better.

The marketing department also favors a large inventory, because it would like to be able to ship today anything that is ordered tomorrow. Its interest in obtaining and maintaining customers leads it to press for a long product line containing as many interrelated products, models, sizes, shapes and colors as the customer may want to purchase from a single source. Hence a basic conflict between the production and marketing departments usually develops concerning the 'length' of the product line and the composition of inventory.

The finance department looks on 'inventory' as a dirty word. When sales drop, this department wants to reduce the amount of capital tied up in the business. It generally finds inventory a convenient place from which to withdraw capital. Hence, it usually presses for reduced inventories during slack periods but may allow inventory to grow during good periods.

Personnel managers, on the other hand, want to maintain the production rate when sales drop in order to retain skilled and trained workers, to reduce hiring and firing costs, and to maintain high morale among the workers. Hence, they want to produce inventory during slack periods. Therefore, they come into conflict with financial management.

Now, the executive has the responsibility of finding an inventory policy that is best for the organization as a whole, not for any particular department. He must consider the effects of a policy on each department, but his evaluation should depend on the overall effect. It is this type of integrating decision that we take to characterize the role of the executive.

Executive-type problems occur at places other than the top level of a business. For example, once the production function is divided, the production manager must integrate and coordinate the activities of the various functions reporting to him: maintenance, quality control, procurement, and so on. There are not only functions, but plants and regions to be coordinated. In effect, then, we consider an executive-type decision to be one that involves putting together the activities of parts of an organization in such a way that the overall operation comes as close as possible to attaining the organization's objectives.

Now let us return to the earlier remark that, during the era of mechanization, science was not applied to executive-type problems in any organized way. Both the executive and the scientist had a reason for this.

The first industrial revolution took place gradually: in fact, it was an evolution rather than a revolution, and it is still continuing. As a consequence, industries grew slowly enough for executives to grow with them. Because of the continuity and gradualness of development, executives could rely on their judgment and past experience to guide them through new problems. The new problems were seldom very different from the old, and so the executives felt no great need for outside assistance.

On the other hand, in the 1920's and 1930's, as the executive function came into increasing importance, scientists found themselves in one of the most underpaid professions in society. They had to find status satisfaction in noneconomic symbols. Consequently, they relied heavily for status on the 'purity' of their research, that is, on the lack of their involvement with practical problems, particularly ones involving the profit motive in any way. They rationalized their position by arguing that practical problems were not as difficult and hence not as challenging as pure research problems. For this reason engineers were looked down upon by the scientist as an inferior lot. Remnants of these attitudes still remain.

Scientists came into very little contact with executives, compared with today, but this changed during World War II. To examine this, we must turn from an industrial setting to one that is military.

It should be noted first that the military had gone through a completely parallel evolution because of mechanization and hence through the same division of labor and management. Major functional divisions had been made (administration, intelligence, operations and services) and subfunctional divisions as well (e.g., signal, transportation, ordnance, engineer and chemical corps). In short, the industrial revolution was mirrored in the military establishment, except for one important difference. The experience of military executives was not continuous. Two decades had passed between the two world wars and there had been a tremendous change in the technology of warfare during that time. Consequently, with the outbreak of World War II, military executives were confronted with the necessity of waging war with a system with which they had had very little real experience. Under these circumstances, military executives turned to the scientists, who had been closely involved in the technological development, for assistance in the operation of the new system. Some scientists put aside their prejudices against applied research and took up the challenge.

More specifically, starting in 1937 British scientists were asked increasingly to assist military executives in learning how to use the then newly-developed radar to locate enemy aircraft. By 1939 this had become a formal activity. The initial objective was to extend the range over which radar could be used, in order to increase the time between the first warning and the attack by enemy aircraft. The scientists recognized that gains could also be made if the time between the first warning and the deployment of defenses could be reduced. This led to study of the communication system linking the detection centers to the defenses. Attention was first given to physical equipment and communication networks, and later to the personnel and executives involved. As the number of early-warning stations was increased, it was observed 'that there was a substantial variation in performance between them, even when operated by the same group of test operators. At the same time with the spread of the number of stations, there was an ever-growing number of operators, and variations in skill of the operators was suspected of being an important factor in the variation of performance of stations . . .'. Analysis revealed ways of improving the operators' techniques and, in the process, also revealed 'hitherto unappreciated limitations in the network, some of them due to local geographical conditions'. (Crowther and Whiddington, 1947, p. 93.)

The scientists working on different aspects of this problem were brought together in September 1939 to H.Q. Fighter Command and '. . . they were encouraged to regard themselves as part of the Command staffs . . .'. The Section steadily extended its scope of activities beyond radar and its uses and, by the time of the Battle of Britain, was consulted on an ever-widening variety of subjects . . . (p. 93)*.

'By the summer of 1941 . . . it was decided to set up OR Sections very widely in the RAF' (p. 94). Similar developments took place in the British Army and Navy, and in both cases radar instigated the activity. In the Army, OR grew out of the initial inability to use radar effectively in controlling the fire of anti-aircraft weapons. In the course of studying this problem

A new point had emerged. Radar apparatus that worked perfectly in the testing-laboratory often failed to work

* *Ibid.*

properly on the sites where it was erected. Thus the traditional method of proofing equipment did not completely apply to the new apparatus. A new gun-sight behaved in the same way in the workshop as in the battlefield. Thus the scientist who tested it need not leave the workshop. He did not need to inspect it on the battle site . . . This would not work with radar gun-sights, for they were 'temperamental' and were affected by the neighborhood (p. 96).*

To solve this problem, in September 1940 the distinguished British physicist, P. M. S. Blackett decided to

bring together a number of men with good scientific training but without specialist radio knowledge, to study the new problems from a more general point of view. They were to study the performance of gun control equipment in the field, especially during its actual use by the troops against the enemy. The first two members of the group were physiologists, the next two were mathematical physicists, then an astro-physicist, followed by an Army officer, an ex-surveyor . . . The team was later completed with a third physiologist, a general physicist and two mathematicians . . . The group became known as 'Blackett's Circus' (p. 96).*

This type of scientific activity came to be known in Britain as 'Operational Research' because the first studies were devoted to the operational use of radar and were carried out by scientists known as working in radar research. Under this and other names it flourished in the United Kingdom.

In *Three Steps to Victory* (London: Odhams Press, 1959), Sir Robert Watson-Watt, who claims to have launched the first two OR studies in 1937, wrote, 'In January and March, 1942, I made, in my reports on my mission of inspection on the Pacific Coast and in the Panama Canal Zone, urgent representations that OR should be introduced into the departments of the Secretary of War and the Secretary of the Navy in the U.S. I gave specific descriptions of some immediate OR tasks in radar. By 1st April, 1942, decisions to introduce operational research at high level in both "War" and "Navy" had been made and implemented' (p. 204). In the Air Force, it came to be known

* *Ibid.*

as Operations Analysis, and in the Army and Navy as Operations Research and Operations Evaluation.

The activity grew not only in the British and U.S. military services, but in the Canadian and the French as well.

At the end of the war, a number of British operational research workers moved to government and industry and began to spread the 'word'. This extension of the work was largely stimulated by the new types of management problems created by the nationalization of industry that began to take place in Britain and by the need to rebuild large segments of the nation's industrial facilities.

One of the first industrial Operational Research groups to be set up was at the National Coal Board where the Board member for science, Sir Charles Ellis, had previously been responsible for the Army's Operational Research. Electricity and transport (rail and air) were other nationalized industries which very soon began to employ Operational Research workers. The private sector of the economy very soon followed suit, and in particular the steel and textile industries took on their first OR men. A feature of British industry which is not extensively matched in the United States is the cooperative research association which operates for all the firms in a particular industry. These research associations, in particular the British Iron and Steel Research Association, aggressively developed OR.

The early development of this new science was cautious and slow. For some years, most British industries where OR was carried out had only one or two men in this field. During the latter half of the 1950's, the germinating seed burst into full flower and existing OR groups expanded to cope with the greatly increased demand from their firms, and in addition other companies went into the OR activity. British OR is partly dominated by a number of large OR groups. The United Steel Companies group now has over eighty people, the National Coal Board over sixty, British Iron and Steel Research Association, British Petroleum and Richard Thomas & Baldwins all have over forty OR workers. In addition, there are a very large number of medium-sized firms with groups of two or three people, and at the present time it is difficult to think of any single type of industry which has not got OR going on somewhere within it.

In the U.S.A., military research increased at the end of the war and so OR men were retained in the military and many more were added. U.S. industry and government (other than military) were not subjected to the same stimulation as they were in Britain and so they remained indifferent to OR.

It was not until 1950 that OR began to be taken seriously by American industry. It took a second industrial revolution to bring it about. In the late 1940s, the United States began to enter a new technological era (that of automation), in which machines replaced man as a source of control. The first industrial revolution had replaced man by machines as a source of power. Specifically, the electronic computer began to infiltrate industry and government and brought with it a host of new broad systems problems with which executives were not equipped to cope. *Past experience was no longer wholly adequate.* Scientists and engineers, who had spent a decade in military OR, were quick to take the opportunities opening up in industry for them. The industrial executive and the research worker finally came together in an activity that has had a phenomenal growth in a single decade.

In preparing the program for the first conference in the U.S. on OR in industry, which was held at the Case Institute of Technology in Cleveland in 1951, it was almost impossible to find industrial case studies to present to the managers who attended. Military examples had to be relied upon. Today, more than a third of the 500 largest corporations in the United States (listed by *Fortune* in 1960) are using operations research. The Operations Research Society of America, formed in 1953, now has several thousand members, most of whom are employed in industry. In Britain a small Operational Research Club was formed just after the war and in 1954 this became the Operational Research Society, which now has a membership of nearly one thousand. More than twenty other national societies have appeared in Europe, Asia and Africa. A few years ago, the International Federation of Operational Research Societies was formed. International OR meetings have been held in England in 1957 and in France in 1960. More than two dozen academic institutions in the U.S.A. are offering courses on the subject and a number are giving graduate degrees. In Britain universities have been painfully slow in developing OR but some progress has been made at Birmingham, London and Manchester.

So much for the evolution and development of OR. Now let us consider its nature and its essential characteristics.

The essential characteristics of OR

In the story just told, the three essential characteristics of OR were identified. But now we should like to pull them out and spotlight them. They are (1) systems orientation, (2) the use of interdisciplinary (or mixed) teams, and (3) the adaptation of scientific method. We will consider each in turn.

Systems orientation

The basic idea involved here is one that is generally accepted in principle by most managers and research men, but it is seldom followed in practice. The idea is that the activity of any part of an organization has some effect on the activity of every other part. It is a principle, which like Newton's laws of gravity, connects each part of a system to every other part. Therefore, in order to evaluate any decision or action in an organization, it is necessary to identify all the significant interactions and to evaluate their *combined* impact on the performance of the organization as a whole, not merely on the part originally involved.

This orientation is quite contrary to what might be called the 'natural' inclination of researchers or managers which is to cut a very complex problem 'down to size', and isolate it from its environment. That is, we tend to eliminate aspects of a problem which make it difficult to solve, and thereby we reduce it to one that can be handled by 'standard' techniques or by judgment based on experience. The system's orientation, on the other hand, moves in the opposite direction; it deliberately expands and complicates the statements of problems until all the significantly interacting components are contained within it.

The term 'significant' is important here, because not all interactions in a system are significant and measurable. In physics, for example, we know in principle that when we brush a speck of dust from our coat, the sun is 'moved', but not to any significant or measurable extent. Therefore, we can ignore it. Consequently, when dealing with a system, the components treated must be selected with an eye to their significance and the measurability of their interaction.

Put another way, this approach consists of covering the entire area under the manager's control and not of concentrating on some special region in this area. Not only does the inquiry go to all the limits of his course, but it examines the effects of policies made outside this area on the activity in the area. This provides the manager in many cases with a basis for initiating inquiries at a higher level into policies which seem to be affecting his performance adversely.

This principle of research, like many others, is better understood by illustration than by abstract and general discussion. So let us consider two industrial case studies in which we can observe the principle in operation.

The company involved in this study had five factories which produce a basic raw material. The output of these plants is shipped to fifteen plants, also owned by the company, which fabricate a wide variety of products. Some of the fabricating plants have considerable overlaps in the products they turn out.

The company spent millions of dollars each year in shipping the raw material from the five to the fifteen plants. Its management wanted a study performed to determine how this shipping could be programmed so as to minimize these costs. This was a 'standard' problem, which could easily have been solved by 'standard' techniques.

When the researchers began collecting information on the output of these five raw-material plants and the requirements of the fabricating plants, they observed that the output of the former plus the material which was purchased from outside sources did not permit many of the fabricating plants to operate at capacity. They then inquired whether the cost of fabrication in each of the fifteen plants depended on the percent of capacity at which they operated. It did, and the effect of unused capacity on production costs varied from plant to plant. In this way the team discovered that the original problem was too restrictive: that is, in shipping metal not only should transportation costs be taken into account, but also the effect on production costs of the distribution of idle capacity resulting from the shipments. Analysis showed that far greater reductions in these production costs could be obtained than in transportation costs and, most important for our purposes here, that a reduction in transportation costs obtained without regard to its effect on production costs would increase the latter by considerably more than the reduction in transportation costs.

Methods were developed for reducing the sum of these two costs and put into operation: but while doing so exploratory studies revealed that the effect of unused capacity on production costs depended on how production was scheduled. Consequently, a second study was initiated on completion of the first to determine how to schedule each plant so as to minimize the sum of these and other production costs. The application of the results of this study required adjusting the costs of idle capacity used in the first problem, but this was an easy adjustment to make.

The study of production scheduling revealed that the cost of production and the time required to fill an order were very sensitive to the mix of sizes and types of items held in semi-finished inventory. Further exploration revealed that changing the stage at which semi-finished inventory was held could yield further saving. Hence, inventory policies were also incorporated into the study.

What we see here is a logical and systematic expansion of the study to include all aspects of the production process, the domain of the managers sponsoring the study. The output of this broad approach is an integrated control system over all aspects of the managers' activity.

The second study began several years ago when one of the major commercial airlines in the United States approached the OR group at the Case Institute of Technology and expressed an interest in trying OR on a small scale in order to determine whether or not the company should go into it in a big way. Management had already selected a problem for study which was felt to be simple enough to be done quickly and at low cost, and the solution of which could readily be evaluated in quantitative terms.

The problem involved the training of stewardesses, of whom the company employed approximately one thousand. Most of these girls left the airline before they had given two years of service, primarily to get married. This turnover was not completely undesirable because stewardesses tend to get stale with the passage of time and excessive exposure to passengers. When they first come on duty they are filled with enthusiasm and provide a high quality of service, but as time goes on they become bored and the service deteriorates. Because of the high rate of attrition, the airline had a continuous need to recruit and train additional stewardesses.

The company had set up a stewardess training school. It was capable of conducting three classes of fifty girls each. Actual training took five and a half weeks. An additional half-week was required for outfitting; a week was required to bring the girls from their homes to school and another was required to get them to their bases after training. This made for a total of eight weeks 'lead time'.

The company wanted to know how often it should run a class and how large the classes should be. On examination it became apparent that this was a familiar problem in production and inventory control. The conversion of a young lady (the raw material) into a stewardess (the finished product) by training (the production process) has associated with it an inventory carrying cost (the salary paid to excess girls whose available time for work is not completely used), shortage costs (those associated with emergency measures or cancellations of flights arising out of shortage of stewardesses), and setup costs associated with preparing the school for a class. The problem then, was one of determining the size and frequency of 'production runs' so as to minimize the sum of these costs, that is, to find the economic 'lot sizes'.

The appropriate mathematical analysis was applied to this familiar problem and it was solved, yielding a set of tables which the school administrator could use to conduct his operation in an optimal way. The savings indicated were fairly impressive.

Now this may sound like the end of the story, but it is only the beginning. In the course of the research, it was necessary to determine how sensitive the cost of running the school was to the accuracy of the forecasts for future requirements. It turned out to be quite sensitive; so much so that a slight increase in the average error of these forecasts would more than wipe out the savings that were indicated. Therefore, it was suggested to management that a study be made of the forecasting procedure to develop a way of keeping it in control. Permission was granted.

The forecasts were generated by what appeared to be a very simple and straightforward procedure. A separate forecast was prepared at each base in the system and these were totalled to obtain the system's requirements. A base is a home station at which stewardesses (and the male members of the crew) are administered. If a stewardess completes her day's work away from her base (even if at another base), her living and local transportation expenses are paid on a *per diem* basis. If she returns to her home base, she is on her own. *Per diem* expenses are a major component of the company's operating expenses.

The stewardess administrator at each base receives a planned flight schedule two months in advance. It shows which flights are to be provided with stewardesses at that base. (Only minor changes are made in these schedules during the intervening two months.) Consequently, the administrator can easily calculate the number of stewardess flight hours which he must provide. He divides the results by the average number of hours flown in the preceding month per stewardess. This yields an estimate of the total number of girls that he will need. He then subtracts from the number of stewardesses he has on hand the number who will leave in the next two months (two-months' notice is required) and adds the number he has 'on order' from classes then in session. By comparing the total requirement with what he will have two months later he determines how many to order.

This forecasting procedure seems to be very simple since it involves very little uncertainty. But on closer inspection it turns out to suffer from a peculiar type of ailment called 'positive feedback'. It leads to continuous deterioration of the system's performance. For example, suppose that a base administrator must supply 1,000 hours of flying time and that the average hours flown last month was 60 per stewardess. Then 1,000/60, or 16.5 stewardesses are required. Hence the administrator must round off the result and, of course, he does so upwards to 17. In the next period, 17 girls fly 1,000 hours or an average of 59 hours. Then, if 1,000 hours are involved in the next time around, the requirement is computed as 1,000/59, or 16.9 girls, which is again rounded off to 17. If in the next period 1,005 hours are again required, the estimated need will turn out to be 17+, and 18 girls are estimated to be required. In this example, in which all the obscuring details are removed, it can be seen how utilization of the stewardesses decreases even when there is little or no change in requirements, because of rounding off. It was not easy to see in the actual situation because of obscuring details but a detailed examination of several years' history showed that such a decrease in utilization had in fact occurred.

The research team therefore proposed a study to determine the maximum possible average number of flying hours per stewardess that could be obtained so that this number could be used in preparing forecasts. Management agreed and the work continued.

The union contract established a maximum number of flying hours per month, say, 100. (We are not free to use the actual figures here for security reasons, but we will use ones which do not seriously distort the order of magnitude of the real problem.) This maximum cannot be realized for two reasons: first, suppose that all flights are 8 hours long. A girl cannot fly 100/8, or 12.5 flights, so again we must round off, but this time down to 12. Thus, 4 hours are 'scrapped'. A certain amount of scrap is unavoidable in such a system.

Secondly, a girl is not permitted to leave on a flight whose scheduled time, when added to the amount she has already flown that month, exceeds 100 hours. Therefore, if she had been scheduled for 100 hours and one flight took more than the scheduled time, she would have to miss one or more of her scheduled flights. Since such delays are quite common, a buffer must be provided against them.

Taking these two factors into account, the maximum possible average flying hours per stewardess were calculated, but only after some very complex mathematics was used. Let us say that the maximum turned out to be 92 hours. The average then being obtained was considerably lower. Therefore a scheduling procedure had to be developed which would realize the theoretically-computed maximum. Such a procedure was developed and taken to management for approval.

The personnel manager objected on the grounds that although regulations permitted the new procedure, the girls would not stand for it. He argued that the increased amount of flying would result in a decrease in job satisfaction and, consequently, the girls would reduce their stay with the company. The only evidence he had to support his view, however, was his 'intimate' knowledge of the girls obtained over many years of working with them. He was willing, however, to allow us to investigate his argument. It turned out to be quite easy to do so. To explain how it was done, we must first explain how the girls obtained their flight assignments each month.

The stewardess administrator at each base combines flights into monthly assignments and posts these on a bulletin board. The senior stewardess at the base has first choice. The next senior girl makes the second choice, and so on. Therefore, using several year's data, a plot of flying hours was made against seniority. If the personnel manager had been correct, the more senior girls would have selected assignments with fewer flying hours. No relationship was found between flying hours and seniority, but there was a relationship between time at the home base and seniority. The girls clearly preferred to spend their time-off at their bases. Consequently, the scheduling procedure which had been developed was revised to increase the average amount of time-at-home by a significant percentage. This required only a very small reduction in average flying time, about one hour per month. An additional bonus was obtained. We found a way to schedule free days more regularly than they had been in the past.

The new scheduling procedure was accepted by management. Again the problem may seem to be at an end, but not quite. In about 6 per cent of the cases the girl assigned to a flight does not appear either because of a delayed in-coming flight or because of illness. Consequently, a certain number of 'reserves' are required at each base to cover these shortages. How many reserves should there be?

To understand this problem consider the following two hypothetical airlines. The first has one stewardess at each of 1,000 bases; the other has all of its girls at one base. The first airline obviously requires 1,000 reserves, one at each base, unless girls are flown specially between bases. The one-base airline requires only a few reserves. Then why not have one-base? The answer lies in the fact that as the number of bases decreases, the amount of time spent away from the base at company expense increases. For example, a girl based in Chicago on the New York to Miami run would be on permanent *per diem*.

Therefore, to determine how many reserves the system should have, one must first determine how many bases there should be, where they should be located, and how flights should be assigned to them for staffing so that the sum of the relevant costs is minimized. But now two other problems immediately become involved.

The first arises from the fact that (for good reasons) the airline will not change part of the crew at a time. The crew must be replaced as a whole. Therefore, the solution to the base problem must consider the effects on the male members of the crew as well as on the stewardesses. The male crew members are more numerous and costly and operate under different conditions than do the stewardesses.

Secondly, bases have other than administrative functions; they also house the principal aircraft repair and maintenance facilities and staff. Consequently, this aspect of operations must also be taken into account in selecting base locations and in determining which flights should be assigned to which bases.

Although the study went further, we think we have gone far enough to make our point. What originally appeared to be a simple and isolated problem turned out to be interconnected with almost all other operating problems of the airline. With expansion of the problem the solutions to the parts could be interrelated to assure best overall performance. This avoided a 'local' improvement which might result in overall loss of efficiency.

By now, you may be concerned over the apparent endlessness of such research. When does it end and when can the results be put into operation? As each part of such a study is completed, its results can be put into immediate operation as long as precautions are taken to prevent disruption of other activities. Subsequent findings may require going back and adjusting previous solutions, and they usually do. In this way the study can pay as it goes and frequently can more than justify the next steps in the enlargement of its scope.

Our answer still leaves the question: does such a project ever end? Of course it does. Either, (1) it reaches the limits of the control exercised by the managers to whom the researchers report, or (2) it reaches a point where further research does not promise enough pay-off to justify continuation, or (3) more fruitful areas of research successfully compete for the researchers' time.

Put briefly, all the interrelated problems uncovered by the systems approach do not have to be solved at the same time, but each must be solved with a prospective and retrospective eye on the others if maximum improvement in overall performance is to be obtained. Application of research findings need not wait until all the interrelated problems are solved. These results can be applied at points in the work where there is assurance of no deleterious affects outside of the domain which has been studied. For example, in the airline study it was possible to use the procedure for scheduling the stewardess training school before going on. However bad the forecasts of demand might be, the procedure assured lowest operating cost, given the forecast. In the metal shipment problem it was possible to allocate metal as soon as costs of unused facilities had been determined, before conducting the study of how to reduce these costs through scheduling.

In general, implementable results come within the first few months of a study and thus provide a basis on which management can evaluate continuation and expansion of the study.

The nature of the system orientation is very effectively summed up in a statement reported to have been made by a British officer during World War II: 'These boys won't even use a soldering iron until they know the whole of the policy of the Pacific war' (p. 116).*

Now to the second essential characteristic of OR.

Interdisciplinary teams
The mixed team arose out of necessity. During the early years of the introduction of OR there was a great shortage of all kinds

* *Ibid.*

of scientists. Physicists, chemists and engineers found ready employment in the technical fields of war-making. Mathematicians and statisticians were taken into statistical sampling and quality control. The output of biologists and zoologists was restricted because there was no military market for their specialties. Consequently, the military operations research groups had to build up their staff by acquisition rather than by selection.

However, out of this necessity came a recognition that the mixed team as such was valuable, and in order to understand why, it is necessary to go back into the history of science.

Most of us think of science as dating back to the Greeks or at least to the Renaissance. The fact is, however, that science only came to be identified as a separate activity about a century ago. Until then the entire domain of human knowledge was subsumed under philosophy.

It is estimated that, until about A.D. 1700, it was possible for one man to know all there was to know about what is now called science. The study of nature expanded tremendously in the eighteenth century. Consequently it was no longer possible for one man to be expert in both traditional philosophy and the growing area of natural studies. As a result natural philosophy, as it was called, began to be distinguished increasingly from philosophy. Finally, in about the middle of the nineteenth century the breach was made official when natural philosophy began to be known as natural science and universities began to divide themselves organizationally into these two parts. The fact that the advanced student in science is still more frequently called a Doctor of Philosophy than a Doctor of Science, is a remnant of our past. Early in the second half of the nineteenth century, because of its growth, natural science had to be further subdivided into physics and chemistry. A bit later, largely stimulated by the development of evolutionary theory, the life sciences came into their own. The more radical universities created departments to house such studies. In the latter part of the century psychology was being born and it too began to gain departmental status, a process that continued well into this century and also in this century we have seen the development of the social sciences. As already indicated, the various engineering disciplines were being organized simultaneously and in parallel with the development of scientific disciplines.

An interesting and important thing about this development is that it seems so logical that we interpret the branches of science as types of reality. That is, we have come to assume that nature is organized the same way that universities are. Nothing could be further from the truth. For example we speak of physical problems, chemical problems, medical and biological problems, psychological problems, social problems, political and economic problems as though we found problems so categorized in nature. In fact there are only problems; the various disciplinary adjectives merely describe different ways of studying them.

For example, a manager rises and leaves the room during a meeting. A physicist could explain this in terms of the resultant of forces operating within and on the human body and he could write equations describing the motion. The chemist could explain the act in terms of chemical changes in the body that produce impulses sent along the nerve net and subsequent contraction and expansion of muscles. The biologist might explain the act by saying the individual had to go to the lavatory. The psychologist might explain it in terms of fatigue or boredom. The sociologist might explain it in terms of a sense of alienation from the group, and so on.

In any simple situation it may be clear which of the alternative ways of viewing a phenomenon is best relative to the viewer's purposes. But when situations become complex, as they do in organized man–machine systems, it becomes increasingly unclear as to what way (or ways) a problem should be looked at. It becomes necessary to look at the problem in many different ways to determine which one or which combination of 'disciplinary' approaches is the best.

Consider, for example, the following story which is reported to be based on the truth. We use it rather than others which we could use and which we know to be true because of its brevity and the effectiveness with which it illustrates the point.

The manager of a large office building was confronted by a growing number of complaints from his tenants about the elevator service. They said they had to wait too long for an elevator. The manager consulted a firm of engineers which specialized in the design of elevator systems. The engineers carried out some time studies which justified the complaints; they showed that the average waiting time for elevators was greater than it should be. They informed the manager that there were three possible ways of improving the situation: by adding elevators, by replacing some of the existing elevators by faster ones, and possibly by 'banking' the elevators, that is, assigning each elevator to serve only a specific subset of floors. The manager asked the firm to evaluate the alternatives and come up with cost estimates.

A while later the results were brought in. The first two alternatives turned out to require an expenditure that the manager did not feel was justified by the earnings of the building. The third alternative did not turn out to yield enough reduction of waiting time. The manager was unhappy with the alternatives and so asked for time to think them over and decide what to do.

As so frequently happens when a manager finds himself confronted with an apparently unsolvable problem, this manager decided to discuss the problem with some of his subordinates. Included in this group was a young psychologist who worked in the employment office which handled the various types of personnel required to operate and maintain a large building. As the manager explained the problem to the small group that had been assembled, the young man expressed surprise at the problem. He said he could not understand why white-collar workers who were known to waste considerable time each day, would object to waiting a very short time. No sooner had he expressed this disbelief than he thought he saw the explanation. While tenants were wasting time in their offices they were doing something else which, though unproductive, was pleasant. But while waiting for an elevator they were much like the proverbial bump on a log. At this the young man's face lit up and he excitedly blurted out a suggestion. The manager took it up and a few days later, after a small expenditure, the problem had been solved. The young man had suggested that large mirrors be put up on the walls in all elevator lobbies. The mirrors obviously gave the women who were waiting something to do, and the men were occupied by staring at the women without appearing to do so.

The truth of this story is not important, but the point that it makes is important. The psychologist had looked at exactly the same problem as had the engineers but he had seen it differently because of his training and interests. In this particular case, his way turned out to be better. Of course, the problem was solved by changing the objective; this no longer was to cut down waiting time but to make it seem less. Let us cite briefly another case in which we have been personally involved.

A major oil company was concerned about the large number of new service stations which it put up each year and which turned out to be unprofitable. To help to solve this problem, the company called on a group of psychologists to conduct motivation research on a sample of service station customers. A good deal of time and money later, a report was issued that made as fascinating reading as a work by Freud. Although it disclosed associations by the customer between such things as the attendant-image and the father-image, it provided practically nothing that could be translated into procedures that would enable the company to construct more profitable stations.

In desperation the company called on an OR group for assistance on the same problem. A team of three, consisting of a physicist, an economist, and a chemical engineer, was assigned to the job.

Company personnel and the consulting psychologists had identified thirty-five variables on which they believed sales volume at a service station to depend. Their forecasting equation contained all of these variables. The physicist in the OR team objected to dealing with such a large number of variables. At his suggestion, the team decided to select only one variable for initial study. The obvious choice was 'traffic'. The team developed a rather obvious way to study traffic, but it was a way which had not previously been used.

They observed that there were sixteen ways to pass through a typical intersection (four entries multiplied by four exits, allowing for turn-backs). For each of a large sample of stations they determined the number of cars using each route, and for each of these the percentage which stopped at the station. The results showed that the same four routes consistently accounted for almost all of the business, and some of these were not the obvious ones. Furthermore they found that with only information about traffic they could better forecast sales volume than could the company with thirty-five variables. But the OR men were not satisfied because they did not understand why some routes through an intersection were more productive than others. It seemed reasonable to assume that it was primarily due to convenience. But how to characterize convenience? One obvious way was to determine the average amount of additional time required by cars in each route if they were to stop at the station. These 'incremental' times were measured at a large number of intersections. The additional time required and the percentage of cars in each route that stopped turned out to have a 'beautiful' relationship. The team then formulated the theory that the prime determinant in service station selection by customers was the amount of time they expected to lose by stopping. Subsequent research supported the theory which was then converted into a way of selecting sites and designing stations to go on them.

Note that in this case the fundamental cause that was eventually uncovered (expected lost time) was psychological in character, but that it was discovered by study of overt behavior by non-psychologists.

To repeat the moral of the elevator and service-station cases: in complex systems we usually cannot predict in advance which of the possible scientific view-points is likely to be the most profitable. Therefore, we should try as many approaches as possible so that we can select that one or combination of approaches that best fit the circumstances. This can only be done by a team of researchers who come from different disciplines or who are familiar with, respect, and know how to use the approaches of disciplines other than their own.

No team can feasibly contain every point of view. It is important, therefore, to use researchers who will subject their work to as wide a critical review by representatives of other disciplines as possible.

Now for the last characteristic: OR's use and adaptation of the scientific method.

OR's method
When we think of scientific research we naturally associate the experimental method with it. Unfortunately, the kinds of

systems with which OR must deal do not lend themselves to laboratory study. (Recall the difficulties with radar.) Furthermore, these systems are generally difficult and frequently impossible, to manipulate and control in their natural environment for experimental purposes. Even where experimentation can be conducted and may succeed, the risk to the company is usually prohibitive. For example, most companies could not use different pricing policies in different regions without alienating their customers. In the relatively few cases where experiments can be performed without damaging the system they are usually too costly or time-consuming.

At first glance these restrictions on the use of the experimental method may seem like an insurmountable handicap to OR. But on reflection we recall that one of the first physical sciences, astronomy, was in much the same position. The astronomer cannot bring the solar system into the laboratory or manipulate it in its natural environment (yet). Nevertheless he has developed a theory that is well supported by observation and which can be used to predict precisely. In the astronomer's method we can find the basic idea behind the methodology of OR.

Since the astronomer cannot manipulate the system he studies, he builds a *representation* of it. This he calls a 'mathematical model'. It represents the structure of the real system in quantitative terms. Models can be manipulated and analyzed more easily than the real system and hence permit the scientist, in effect, to carry on vicarious experimentation. He can systematically vary some properties of the system, holding others constant and in this way determine how the system as a whole would be affected if the changes actually did occur. In fact, he simulates the real life alteration and experiments in abstract terms.

The OR team constructs and uses mathematical models in the study of organized man—machine systems and hence carries out experiments in this symbolic way. These models may be very difficult to construct and may turn out to be very complicated mathematical expressions. Underlying this complexity, however, is a relatively simple structure. All OR models take the form of an equation in which a measure of the system's overall performance (P) is equated to some relationship (f) between a set of controlled aspects of the system (C_i) and a set of uncontrolled aspects (U_j). Thus expressed symbolically, the basic form of all OR models is

$$P = f(C_i, U_j)$$

In words, this statement says that performance depends upon significant controlled and uncontrolled aspects of the system. Now let us consider each of these components of a model.

The development of an adequate measure of the system's performance may be a very difficult—if not the most difficult—aspect of the research. It must reflect the relative importance of, and conflict between the multiplicity of objectives involved in every executive-type decision. These objectives are of two types:

(1) those which involve *retaining* things of value which are already available; to minimize inputs (expenditure, in the generalized sense); and

(2) those which involve *obtaining* things of value which are not yet possessed; to maximize outputs (income, in the generalized sense).

The 'things' involved may be resources (for example, time, money and energy), or states of the system (for example, share of the market, product leadership, and public acceptance).

In developing a measure of performance it is necessary, first, to develop a measure of the degree to which each objective is obtained. These are called measures of *efficiency*. But the scales used in these measures may not be the same. For example, the scale used to measure the degree to which the objective—to minimize cost—is obtained would be monetary; the scale used to measure the degree to which the objective—to maximize customer service—is obtained may be (delivery) time. It is necessary, therefore, to find a way of expressing units on the different scales of efficiency on some one common scale. The scale usually employed for this purpose in an industrial context is itself a monetary one. When the various measures of efficiency are transformed on to one scale and are then consolidated into a single measure, the resulting measure is one of *effectiveness*. It takes all the objectives into account.

The units on the effectiveness scale may not all be of equal value. For example, to a starving man the first dollar or pound is more valuable than is the second. Similarly, the first million dollars or pounds of income may be worth more to a company than is the second. It may be necessary, therefore, to take into account the value of the units on the effectiveness scale; that is, to transform the measure of effectiveness into a measure of value. Techniques for transforming one scale into another and for evaluating the units on a scale are now highly developed but a considerable amount of research may be required to apply them appropriately.

The controlled variables may include such things as the size and frequency of production runs, the number of different products made, the price of each, departmental budgets, and the number of salesmen employed. The values of each of the controlled variables can be set by management. The problem is to determine the values at which to set them.

Among the uncontrolled variables may be such things as competitive prices, the cost of labor and raw material, the location of customers, and the amount of demand for each product. These are factors which, at least within the context of the problem, are not subject to management's control.

The basic model may have to be supplemented by a set of statements which reflect limitations or restrictions on the possible values of the controlled variables. For example, the amounts allocated to departments in a budget cannot exceed the total amount available. Nor can the amount of product shipped to consumers be greater than the amount available. These restrictions are expressed in a set of supplementary equations or inequations (i.e. statements involving the relationship 'must be less than' or 'greater than').

So far we have discussed the derivation of a model by means of mathematical and statistical analysis. In some cases, however, the mathematics breaks down before the sheer complexity of the real life situation. In these cases the OR scientist behaves just as his colleague in a laboratory would behave, namely he experiments. In fact, if it were possible, all OR would involve real life experimentation. However, the problems of the industrial executive are not those in which real life experimentation can be carried out since he is faced, not with trial and error, but trial and disaster. Consequently, the OR worker has to find some way of experimenting in an abstract form, such that there is a close relationship between the make up of his experiment and the real life situation in such a way that the real life situation is not affected by his experiments. These methods are called simulation.

Let us take a very simple example. Suppose we want to know the chance that a hand of cards at bridge will contain all four aces. In this particular case the problem is soluble mathematically, but if we assume that we have not got the mathematical equipment necessary to solve this problem theoretically the obvious thing to do would be to deal out a great number of bridge hands and find out how many of them contained all four aces. If we did this a sufficiently large number of times we would take the proportion of successes as being our estimate of the chance of four aces appearing. Suppose now that we could not lay our hands on a pack of cards and were not able to solve the mathematics of the problem. One obvious way of estimating the result would be to place 48 white balls and four black balls in a hat and take out four random samples of 13. If we then replaced the balls and carried on with this experiment we could take the proportion of times which we get four black balls as being the estimate of the proportion of bridge hands, which would contain four aces. As will be seen, we have now moved away from the direct experiment (i.e. taking the real life situation of a pack of cards and representing it by a bag of balls). In fact, we have simulated real life and carried out an experiment.

This simple example illustrates what we mean by the term simulation and it is a very powerful method at the disposal of the OR worker. By this simulation the OR worker can carry out experiments in exactly the same way as his colleague in the experimental sciences and it is simulation which forms the bridge between OR and the other experimental sciences.

By simulating an industrial decision-making situation, we can determine exactly or approximately those values of the controlled variables which optimize the performance of the system. Hence, however it is derived, whether by mathematics or statistics or by simulation, the basic form of all OR models is:

$$P = f(C_i, U_j)$$

Once a model has been constructed to represent a problem situation a solution is sought. In order to obtain a solution one seeks those values of the controllable variables (C_i) that maximize or minimize—whichever is appropriate—the measure of performance (P). The extraction of a solution may be accomplished either by conducting experiments on the model—that is, by simulation, or by mathematical analysis. In either case, the solution yielded consists of one equation for each controllable variable of the form

$$C_1 = f_1(U_j)$$
$$C_2 = f_2(U_j)$$
$$C_3 = f_3(U_j)$$

etc.

The 'optimizing' values of the controlled variables are expressed as functions of the values of the uncontrolled variables. These equations are called 'decision rules'.

In formulating the model the researchers must state explicitly what managers consider to be under their control, and what is not. The researchers do not take management's statements for granted but investigate their justification. In many cases it is found that variables considered to be uncontrollable can be brought under control and restrictions on controllable variables can be lifted. In so doing a better solution can often be obtained than would be otherwise. For example, consider the case of a company that produces a material used in many production processes. The company maintains a large number (over one hundred) of warehouses in industrial centers from which manufacturers pick up their requirements. The volume of sales of the company was growing steadily but so was the field inventory, and it was doing so at what management considered to be an alarming rate. They tried to reduce field inventories by establishing limits on stored quantities but this only resulted in the demand by warehouses on the factory for more frequent and more rapid delivery. This demand resulted in such an increase in factory inventory that total inventory was not affected. Management then made efforts to introduce economic order quantities on the warehouses and economic lot sizes on the factory, but this resulted in only minor improvements. At this point an OR group was brought in.

When a model of the problem was formulated it became apparent that the growth of inventory was due to the small purchase quantities of the customers. Since the material spoiled easily in humid environments, users did not want to store large quantities. Discounts which the company offered for large purchases did not compensate for the losses associated with stocking the material and so had little effect on the customers.

The model revealed another critical 'uncontrolled' variable, the amount of lead time the customer gives the warehouse in filling an order. The company had always accepted customers calling at the warehouse, placing an order and picking up the desired material immediately. By manipulating the model it could be shown that the longer the lead time provided by customers in filling orders, the less inventory would be required. In the extreme, if orders were placed far enough in advance, no matter how small they were, production and stocking could be conducted 'to order'. In addition, by further manipulation of the model it was possible to determine how much it was worth to the company to increase this lead time. This led to the recommendation of a price discounting plan in which the discount offered increased with lead time provided by the customer. Such a plan did not require the customer to stock any more of the item than he had previously, only to inform the warehouse in advance what he wanted when. The plan was installed and produced the desired effect: it reduced inventories and costs despite the additional discount offered.

Another case in which a solution was obtained by making an 'uncontrollable' variable controllable involved a company which produced about 3,000 distinct products most of which were sold in small volume at an unacceptably low profit or loss. A relatively small number of high-volume profitable items carried the business but their production costs were increasing because of the need to shorten production runs in order to turn out the many short-runs of the less profitable items: the problem, as management saw it, was to schedule production more effectively. But the OR team saw the problem as one involving elimination of unprofitable products from the line. They were informed that this was not possible because these poor items were ordered by customers who were heavy consumers of the profitable items and, hence, if the product line were shortened, the sale of profitable items would suffer. General management, marketing management, and the salesmen were unanimous in this opinion, an opinion which made 'the product line' an uncontrollable variable. They also precluded increasing the price of the unprofitable items because, they argued, this would throw their business to competitors who were willing to supply these items at a lower cost and who could afford to do so since they enjoyed a larger volume of sales of these items.

The researchers obtained information on the profitability or loss associated with each product at the current level of sales. They then examined the salesmens' pay which consisted of a base salary plus commission based on dollar volume of sales. A new salesman compensation plan was designed which would yield the same income to salesmen but which was based on the profitability of sales. This system provided no commission for sale of unprofitable items, but increased commissions for the sale of profitable ones. Now, it was argued, if the sale of the poor items was necessary to get sales of the good ones, they would continue to be obtained at no loss to the salesmen. But if they were not necessary, the salesmen would be wasting their time in getting them. Management accepted this argument and the plan. Its installation resulted in the discontinuation of sales of many of the unprofitable items with no decrease in sales of the profitable items. The salesmen found they could control the items sold, once they were motivated to do so.

Now we must consider a difficulty in dealing with models of problem situations with which the astronomer is not faced. The values of uncontrolled variables in organized systems are subject to change over time. As these values change so must the optimizing values of the controlled variables. Thus, in a very real sense, there is no such thing as *a* solution to an executive-type problem. The research must yield a *procedure* which is capable of providing the optimal solution under any specific set of feasible conditions. Therefore, the output of OR is not only a solution relative to an existing set of circumstances, but it must also contain a procedure for (1) determining when significant changes have occurred in the system, and (2) adjusting the solution to take these changes into account. The adequacy of the solution of course, depends on how accurately the model represents the real system. Hence both the model and the solution derived from it must be carefully tested and evaluated. This usually involves some small scale testing of the results in the real world, a kind of pretest or pilot operation.

There is one remaining essential characteristic of OR's methodology: its concern and involvement in the implementation of its results. OR can only partially test its results against the past or, as indicated, in the laboratory. Consequently, the real test of results must come in their application in the real world. For this reason OR workers must translate their results into a set of instructions for management and operating personnel. These instructions should indicate in detail who is to do what, when and how they are to do it. In effect, the researchers must provide a *program* which is similar to the programs prepared for electronic computers. Only with such detailed instructions can assurance be had that the results of the research are being fairly tested.

There is a case in which the instruction prepared for stock clerks involved the expression '$\sqrt{2}$'. The clerks were unfamiliar with the square root sign and interpreted it to mean 'divided by two'. This resulted in a distortion of the research findings. This incident emphasizes not only the need for detailed instructions but also the need for expressing them in a vocabulary that is familiar to those who must follow them.

Despite the most thorough advanced planning something almost always comes up in application that was not anticipated. This is another reason why the research team must be involved in the implementation of the findings. OR is *action* research, its objective is not to turn out reports but to improve operations. This cannot be done without becoming directly involved in the operations.

By now some managers will have asked themselves, 'How can a group of scientists and engineers, however ingenious they are come into my organization and learn enough about it to help me solve problems that give me difficulty? It took me years to learn what I know of my company, and I don't know enough to solve such problems.' In effect, each executive feels his problems are different (and usually more difficult) than those confronting any other executive. Familiarity breeds complexity. Even if OR can help others how can it help him?

The executive is right in thinking that his problems are different from anyone else's, but he is wrong in thinking they are different in *every* respect. There are two different ways of looking at problems and, as usual, the Greeks had words for them. They differentiated the *form* and the *content* of problems. Two problems seldom if ever arise which have the same content but there are relatively few forms which problems can assume. *About eight different forms account for almost all the problems that ever confront a manager.* An understanding of this distinction, then, is essential for an understanding of how OR can help an executive.

Most managers will know that the equation

$$y = a + bx$$

represents a straight line. The remarkable thing about this recognition is that the person involved does not know what y, a, b or x represents. Therefore the equation is an expression of pure form; it has no content. It gains content only when the symbols are defined and hence given meaning.

Now, when OR men work on an executive problem the necessary knowledge of its content is provided primarily by management and operating personnel. This is supplemented by study of the operations themselves. From the information obtained in these ways the researchers can *abstract* the form of the problem and describe it in a mathematical model. Once this is done, the form can be classified and the appropriate body of mathematical techniques can be brought to bear on its solution. It is in the design of the implementation procedures that the form of the solution is given meaning and is brought back into the real world.

Hence managers, operating personnel, and OR men must work together if meaningful solutions to real problems are to be obtained. Such research must be a joint venture in which management plays a very active role.

Now we have considered how OR developed and what it is, but we have left a rather conspicuous gap: we referred to eight basic forms which account for most management problems, but we did not identify them or offer any evidence for our assertion. We do so in the next chapter.

2 The Form and Content of Problems

IN THIS chapter we maintain that operational research is a unity. By this, we mean that whether it is carried out in steel making or detergent making, shipbuilding or oil refineries, operating broiler farms or operating coal mines, there is a common thread running through all the work undertaken. This thread has two strands. The first is the erection of a working model which is manipulated by the OR worker so as to derive the basis for the most effective action by management; the second strand to this thread is the way in which the problems themselves can be classified.

Forms of problems

There is no unique classification of the set of problems which arise in OR but for each type of classification which we use it will be seen that problems repeat themselves, the same type of problem arising in many diverse industries. Consequently, we put forward the following eight basic forms, which singly or in combination account for most of the problems that confront executives, not because they are the only useful classification but because they are forms which for our present purposes in this particular book and for the particular audience at whom we are aiming this book, are, we feel, the most useful.

The classification of problems is:

1.	Inventory	5.	Routing
2.	Allocation	6.	Replacement
3.	Queuing	7.	Competition
4.	Sequencing	8.	Search

Each form is a theme on which a number of variations can be played. We shall consider the principal themes and illustrate each.

We shall also make a few remarks about the current state of the art and science of handling these problems, but will avoid the technical details that can be found in texts on the subject and to which references are given. You will observe that some mathematical techniques can be used to solve problems of different forms and that several different techniques can be used to solve problems of any particular form.

Let us emphasise that our objective here is not to produce understanding of the mathematical techniques used to solve problems of the types to be discussed, but rather to produce an understanding of the structure of these problems.

Inventory problems

'Inventory' is idle resources, and 'resources' are anything which can be used to obtain something else of value. Men, material, machines, and money are the principal resources with which industrial managers are involved.

For a problem to exist in inventory there must be two types of cost associated with idle resources: (1) a cost which increases as inventory increases, and (2) a cost which decreases as inventory increases.

One cost which increases as inventory does is, of course, the inventory carrying cost. This includes such components as storage costs, obsolescence and spoilage costs, taxes, insurance, and so on.

There are four principal costs which decrease as inventory increases:

1. *Shortage or outage costs:* those associated with either the inability to meet demand or delays in meeting it; for example, the costs of lost customers and sales. As inventories increase, the likelihood of delays in meeting demand decreases.

2. *Setup and takedown costs:* those associated with preparing, processing, and closing out a purchase or production order, and in the case of production, with adjusting the equipment for the new manufacturing operations. The larger the production or purchase quantity, the less frequently orders need be processed and so this cost will decrease as inventory increases.

3. *Purchase price or direct production costs:* quantity discounts reduce price but, if used, lead to larger purchases, and hence larger inventories. Longer production runs generally lead to greater efficiency and hence lower unit cost, but increase inventories.

4. *Labor stabilization costs.* If demand fluctuates and one wishes to minimize inventory it is necessary to vary the production rate and hence increase the costs of hiring, firing and training personnel.

Now an inventory problem can be defined as one in which at least one of each type of cost is involved and where the sum of these costs is affected by either the quantity of the resource acquired per order (e.g. production or purchase quantities), or the frequency of acquisition, or both. The problem, of course, is to select the quantity or frequency of acquisition, or both, so that the sum of the relevant costs is minimized.

In a plant which always manufactures its product in batches of specified size (e.g. in many chemical processes), one usually controls the frequency rather than the quantity of production. A housewife, on the other hand, does not control the time of delivery of milk but she does determine the amount. This was also the case in purchasing steel during the last war. In a typical job shop, on the other hand, both the amount and frequency of production are under management's control.

Inventory problems may appear in a wide variety of contexts other than in the usual production and purchasing areas. We have already cited the operation of a stewardess training center as a problem of this type. It will be recalled that the questions involved were: how often to run a class and how large such a 'production run' should be. If too many stewardesses are 'turned out', the company must pay salaries for service capabilities which are not used, an inventory-carrying cost. If too few stewardesses are turned out, either flights will have to be cancelled or emergency measures will have to be taken, which involve shortage costs. Most training problems are inventory problems. Let us cite a few others.

Several years ago a public utility asked for assistance in determining when to add a turbo-electric generator to its system and how large it should be. Although only one (multi-million dollar) piece of equipment was involved its capacity was subject to choice. Hence both the 'how much' and 'when' questions were asked. If too large a generator is purchased, or if it is obtained too soon, idle capacity results which involves an inventory-carrying cost in the form of depreciation. If too little is purchased, or if it is purchased too late, sales will be lost and the public utility commission responds unfavorably. These result in shortage costs.

The question, 'How much operating capital should a company keep available?' also presents an inventory problem. If too much capital is kept available, earnings from possible investments of the excess are lost, an inventory-carrying cost. If too little is kept available, additional capital will have to be borrowed at premium rates, a shortage cost. There are also setup and takedown costs associated with obtaining loans.

Some of the more complex forms of inventory problems should be mentioned. One of these involves supply systems that operate at several levels. For example, a company may have inventories at factories, field warehouses, and company-owned distributors. Here the inventory questions must be answered in such a way as to minimize the total cost, over all levels. This is called the 'multi-level' inventory problem.

Another common but complex inventory problem arises in determining at what point in a production process inventories should be held, and of what they should consist. The more finished the goods which are held in inventory, the less is the delay in supplying customers, but the greater the carrying costs. The less finished the goods (raw material in the extreme), the longer it takes to fill orders but the less costly it is to carry the stock. Furthermore, forecasting errors for items in stock tend to increase, the more differentiated (finished) the items are.

Related to this last problem is the one involving the number of retail establishments a company should have. The more there are the greater the carrying costs but the fewer sales are lost.

Mathematical techniques for handling inventory problems are very highly developed. They are quite varied in character and depend primarily on the use of the calculus and probability theory, but they also apply matrix algebra (as in linear programming) and the calculus of variations (as in dynamic programming). In some very complex cases where the appropriate models can be constructed but not solved, simulation techniques can be used to obtain a solution. These techniques normally involve the use of an electronic computer. They consist essentially of imitating the operation of the system under varying conditions to find which set of conditions yields the least cost. The literature on techniques of solving inventory problems is very extensive and ranges from the relatively elementary (Magee, 1958) to the very complex (Arrow, Karlin and Scarf, 1958). Most managers would have no trouble with large portions of the former. An extensive review and bibliography of these techniques is provided by Hanssmann (1961).

Allocation problems
These problems fall into three main categories. First we consider the most restricted type, and then, by removing restrictions we describe the other two.

An allocation problem of the first type is defined by the following conditions:
1. There is a set of jobs (of any type) to be done.
2. Enough resources are available for doing all of them.
3. At least some of the jobs can be done in different ways and hence by using different amounts and combinations of resources.
4. Some of the ways of doing these jobs are better than others (e.g. are less costly or more profitable).
5. There are not enough resources available, however, to do each job in the best way.

Therefore, the problem is to allocate the resources to the jobs in such a way that the overall efficiency is maximized; for example, so that total cost is minimized or total profit is maximized.

In the simplest allocation problem of this type each job requires one and only one resource, and there are the same number of jobs and resources. This problem is called the *assignment* problem because it involves assigning one resource to each job. The resource may very well be a person.

There is a cost or profit associated with each combination of job and resource. The problem is to assign the resources so that the total cost of doing the jobs is minimized or profit maximized.

For example, the resources may be empty offices and the jobs may be the housing of men; or the resources may be trucks of different sizes and the jobs may be delivery routes of differing characteristics. Drivers must be assigned to trucks, operators to machines, clerks to particular clerical tasks, classes to rooms.

This type of problem becomes more complex if some of the jobs require more than one resource and if the resources can be used for more than one job. Then the problem involves dividing the resources and jobs appropriately. One of the most familiar examples of this type is the *transportation* problem. For example, there may be a number of empty freight cars available at certain classification yards, and a number are required at various locations. How should each point requiring cars be supplied? Or again if there are a number of plants each producing the same products, from which should the requirements of various customers be filled? In short, most *distribution* problems are of this sort.

In some cases the resources and the jobs are characterized by measures on different types of scale. For example, the jobs may be described as the number of each type of product required. The resources may be the amount of time available on machines of different types. For example, in one plant which produces a pharmaceutical compound and packages it in many different sized containers, there are six packaging machines, each different from the other but most of them are capable of handling several different sizes of containers. The cost of packaging in a certain container differs for each machine. But if the most efficient machine were used in each case, some machines would be overloaded and others would be idle. The preparation of a packaging program is an allocation problem. A similar problem arises in assigning accounts to salesmen.

In many steel works production is 'to order'. There will be a number of different ways in which a given order can be processed (that is, different combinations of machines or order of operations). In most weeks if the best production practice is selected for each order, some machines would be overloaded while others remain idle. The task of the production manager is to make the selection in such a way as to minimize the total cost of production.

The second major type of allocation problem arises when there are more jobs to be done than available resources permit. Hence a selection of jobs must be made as well as a determination of how they are to be done. The familiar 'product-mix problem' is of this type, as for example, in oil refinery operations. Given the demand for each of a wide range of products (all of which cannot be produced at the same time), and the prices at which they can be sold, what combination of petroleum products should be made in what quantities so as to maximize the expected profit?

The problem of how a salesman should divide his limited time among too long a list of accounts is of the same type. Most budgeting problems are also of this type. For example, there are usually many more research and development projects available to a company than it has funds or personnel to carry out.

The third type of allocation problem arises when one has control over the amount of resources and hence can determine what resources should be added, where or what resources should be disposed of. For example, the need to determine where to build a new plant or warehouse creates a problem of this type. Or the decision as to which of several plants to shut down during slack periods is of the same type. Within a plant the same type of problem may arise with respect to determining what types of machines to add or remove from the production line. 'How many salesmen should a company have and how should their territories be selected?' is a question of the same type.

In some allocation problems the cost of doing a job in a particular way does not depend on how the other jobs are done. This is so, for example, where machine time is assigned to production orders. That is, the time required to produce item 1 on machine A does not depend on the time required to produce item 2 on machine B. Much more complicated is the case where the costs or profits expected from one activity depend on what resources are allocated to other activities. Most budgeting problems are of this complex type. The yield of an amount of money spent on marketing, for example, usually depends on how much is spent on research and development and production. Although, there are very highly developed mathematical techniques for handling the former (independent allocation) case, for the latter (interdependent case) there is still a shortage of good techniques.

Most of the techniques used to solve allocation problems are of a type called *mathematical programming*. The various types of programming—linear, nonlinear, stochastic, parametric, and dynamic—differ in the kinds of data which they can handle and the kinds of assumptions they make. The development of these techniques is quite recent; previously there was no feasible way of solving most allocation problems because of the amount of computation involved. Even now, without the help of electronic computers many of them could not be solved in any reasonable time.

For reviews of these techniques see Arnoff and Sengupta (1961), and Dreyfus (1961). Extensive references to other sources are made in these reviews.

Queuing problems

Perhaps the best way of understanding the nature of a queuing problem is by a diagram, and you are referred now to Fig. 1. In this diagram we show the arrival of customers to the end of the

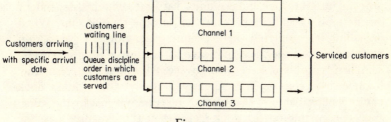

Fig. 1.

queue, the waiting of customers within the queue until they can pass through a service facility, a rate at which the customers can be dealt with through the service facility, and finally, the turning out of serviced customers at the end of the service facility.

We have already started talking in the jargon of queuing theory. The location at which jobs are carried out is a 'service facility'. The jobs arriving to be carried out, regardless of their nature, are 'customers'. If a number of jobs can be worked on at the same time then we say that we have different 'channels' and a 'channel' itself may consist of a 'line' of service points or only one point. The waiting of customers is called a 'queue' and the order in which customers leave the 'queue' for service is called the 'queue discipline'.

The systems described will nearly always have waiting customers, or idle service facilities and/or personnel, with the associated costs. These include loss of business, idle equipment and hence higher depreciation costs and excessive labor costs, and the problem is to minimize the sum of these.

Queuing problems are common both in everyday life and also in industrial processes. A classical application of queuing theory was carried out some years ago by an OR team in the British Iron and Steel Association. For a full description of this, see Eddison and Owen (1953). This problem concerned the docking facilities for unloading iron ore in ports. There is not sufficient space for us to describe this fascinating case study in full, but briefly the problem was as follows:

Ships loaded with iron ore arrive at a port, and the necessary conditions for their being able to berth are that the tide is at the right height and that there are berths of the right kind available. Once these conditions are satisfied, one of the waiting ships can proceed into the dock and can unload at a rate which is dependent on the type of facilities on shore and on the type of ship. When unloading is completed then, assuming the tide is right, a ship can move out of the dock and leave its berth free for a successor. The basic problem here was to see what was the economic balance between having expensive, and possibly idle, dock equipment available so that no waiting time was lost by the ships, and economizing on the dock facilities at the expense of having ships waiting outside the port.

In terms of the description with which we opened this section, this is a straightforward queuing problem. As with most queuing problems, the mathematics to which it gives rise are virtually insoluble. In these cases, solutions are obtained by means of 'simulation' and in this particular example it was possible to show how large ports should be laid out or adapted to minimize total cost.

As they have been described, it is apparent that some inventory problems can also be looked at as queuing problems. Items in stock can be viewed as idle-service facilities waiting for customers, the demand for stock is the arrival of a customer for service and the outage of stock is a queue of customers.

The mathematical theory of queues is highly developed and makes extensive use of probability theory and differential and integral equations. This is no field for the mathematical novice. The best coverage of the theory can be found in Morse (1958), Cox and Smith (1961) and in Syski (1960).

Sequencing problems

In queuing problems the order in which waiting customers are selected for service is usually assumed to be specified. Sequencing problems are concerned with selecting a queue discipline so that some appropriate measure of performance is minimized; for example, the total elapsed time required to service a specified group of waiting customers. This may have to be done under a system of priorities as, for example, when there are due-dates on production orders, and penalties for delay in delivery.

Consider the following very simple example of a sequencing problem. Suppose there are two products to be made, *A* and *B*. Each requires operations on two machines, 1 and 2, and for both products the operations on machine 1 must precede those on machine 2. Now suppose *A* requires two hours on machine 1, and ten hours on machine 2, and that *B's* requirements are six and four hours respectively. Each possibility can be evaluated graphically by a technique called the Gantt chart, named after its inventor. These are shown in Fig. 2.

A graphic comparison of the two possible sequences (*AB* and *BA*) shows that there is a 4-hour difference in the total elapsed time. There can be quite a difference in even such a simple case.

It might seem that this simple graphic technique is all that is required to solve any problem of this type, but such is not the case. If we have ten jobs to sequence over two machines, and all jobs must go over them in the same order, there are approximately 3,700,000 possible sequences. Clearly we cannot graph each of them. Moreover, if more than two machines are involved and the order of jobs over them differs, you can imagine the additional complexity that is created.

Only the very simplest sequencing problems can be solved

by mathematical analysis. In almost every real problem it is necessary to resort to simulation, and even here the amount of work is often prohibitive and only approximate solutions can be obtained. These, however, are usually better than what judgment and intuition can provide. Let us cite one case in which a very extensive simulation was performed.

After two years of intensive study of a very complex job-shop a simulation of the shop operations was programmed on a large computer. The simulation imitated almost every detail of the operations: machine breakdowns, shortages of materials, absenteeism of workers, varying production rates, and so on. On Saturday morning the plant scheduler submitted to the computer a proposed sequence of jobs for the following week. The computer ran the proposed schedule eight separate times. It did this in order to obtain an estimate of the *average* length of time to complete the sequence. (Each run of the same sequence yielded

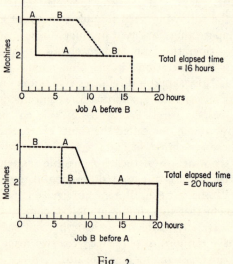

Fig. 2.

different results because of the chance factors. This reflects the fact that the same sequence run in successive weeks in the plant would not take exactly the same time in each instance.) The computer examined the results and modified the schedule in a way that had some chance of improving it. Eight runs of the revised sequence were made. This process was continued for 150 different sequences. The reason 150 sequences were used was that extensive testing had shown that the amount of improvement that could be obtained by running more trial sequences did not justify the computational costs. The best of the 150 trials was selected and used for sequencing the next week's work. The entire process was completed by noon on Saturday.

A good deal of experimental simulation has been conducted on sequencing problems and some general rules for improved, not necessarily optimal, sequencing have begun to emerge. They must be used with caution because they apply only under certain types of conditions. For a review of these findings and a view of the general technical state of sequencing problems see Sission (1961).

Very recently techniques have been developed for handling a variation of the sequencing problem that occurs in planning a construction job or a research and development program. It is concerned with processes which are unique and are performed only once. Some steps in the process must precede others, some may be done simultaneously. The problem is to establish starting times and due-date goals such that the costs of operations are minimized. Penalties for lateness can be taken into account or rewards for finishing early. The two techniques developed to handle this kind of problem are called 'PERT' (see Malcolm *et al.*, 1959) and the 'Critical-Path Method' (see Kelley, 1961).

Kelley lists the following problems to which the critical-path method can be applied.

1. All types of construction and maintenance
2. Retooling program for high-volume production
3. Low-volume production scheduling
4. Scientific missile countdown procedures
5. Budget planning
6. Mobilization, strategic and tactical planning
7. New product launching
8. Assembly and testing of electronic systems
9. Installation, programming, and debugging of computer systems (p. 297).

To apply these techniques information is needed on the sequences required, the duration of each phase, and the costs for each part of the project. The techniques make it possible to determine labor needs, budget requirements, procurement and design limitations and the effects of delays or speed-ups and communication difficulties.

Routing problems

Mathematicians have long amused themselves with very difficult problems which are treated like puzzles. One of the more recent of these is the 'traveling salesman problem'. It is usually formulated somewhat as follows. A salesman has a certain number of cities he must visit. He knows the distance (or time, or cost) of travel between every pair of cities. His problem is to select a route which starts at his home city, goes through each city only once, and returns to his home city in the shortest possible distance (or time or cost).

The problem has two variations. In one, the symmetrical case, the distance (or time or cost) between any two cities, A and B, is the same regardless of the direction of travel (i.e. A to B or B to A). In the more complicated case, the asymmetrical one, for example, the time to travel from A to B (say downhill) may be less than that of traveling from B to A (uphill).

If only two cities are involved there is, of course, no choice. If three cities are involved, one of which is the home base (A), there are two possible routes (ABC and ACB). For four cities there are six possible routes. But for eleven there are approximately 3,700,000 possible routes.

The mathematical problem has been to find a completely general way of solving this problem by analysis rather than by trial and error. The problem has attracted a good deal of attention because it is so simple to state but so difficult to solve. A completely general analytical solution has yet to be found, but completely general numerical solution procedures have been found.

Those working on this problem had no idea that it might have some practical relevance even though it was stated in terms of routing salesmen. A short while ago, however, this type of problem reared its head in an unexpected and very practical way.

The company concerned was producing about twenty different models of kitchen sinks on one continuous assembly line. Some of the models were very much like others; some were quite different. The cost of changing over the assembly line from production of one model to another depended on the nature of these models.

In some cases it could be done quickly and at low cost; in others a good deal of time and money was required. Furthermore, it might take more time to change from model A to model B than from model B to model A. One direction of change might involve eliminating some operations, the other might involve adding some; as, for example, the number of shelves in the cabinet under the sink.

Despite intensive efforts it was not possible to develop a way of selecting an order in which the models should be produced so as to minimize the total cost of change overs. However, a procedure was found which reduced the then current costs by almost a third. Only after this was done did the researchers come to realize that they had been working on the asymmetrical traveling salesman problem, or 'routing problem' as it has now come to be called. The sink models corresponded to cities and the change-over costs corresponded to the costs of travel between cities. A route was sought which led to each model (city) without return to any one.

An elementary discussion of the techniques for handling the routing problem can be found in Churchman, Ackoff, and Arnoff (1957).

Replacement problems

Replacement problems are of two general types: those involving items that degenerate with use or the passage of time, and those which do not, but which die or fail after a certain amount of use or time. Items that deteriorate are likely to be large and costly, for example, machine tools, trucks and ships, generators, and home appliances. Nondeteriorating items generally maintain a fairly level efficiency throughout their lives, but suddenly stop operating completely. These items tend to be small and relatively inexpensive; for example, light bulbs, vacuum tubes, tire tubes, automobile springs, rubber bands and ball-point pen fillers.

We will consider each type of item separately; first, the deteriorating type.

The longer a deteriorating item is operated without preventive or corrective maintenance, the more inefficient its operation usually becomes and hence the unit cost of production increases. In order to keep up its efficiency, maintenance is required and this involves a cost. In addition such items may become obsolete by the appearance on the market of improved items of the same sort. Therefore, the longer the equipment is retained the greater is the cost of maintaining it or the greater is the loss due to the decrease in relative and absolute efficiency.

On the other hand, if the equipment is replaced frequently the investment costs increase. The problem, then, is to determine when to replace such items so that the sum of the operating and investment costs are minimized.

A number of procedures are available for handling problems of this type. In many cases relatively simple applications of the calculus are sufficient. The technique of dynamic programming is perhaps the most generally applicable. These techniques, as well as others applicable to both types of replacement problem, are thoroughly reviewed by Dean (1961).

In the case of nondeteriorating items that die the problem usually consists of determining whether to 'group replace' or not, and if so, how often. Consider two extreme policies. First, replace items only when they fail; that is, individually. The advantage of this policy is that the number of items required is minimized. But failures are relatively frequent and hence the costs associated with them are relatively high. If, on the other hand, all items are replaced in a group before any one of them fails, the costs of failures are minimized but the number of items required is virtually maximized. It is usually less expensive to replace an item if it is one of a group being replaced than if it is only one, but more replacements are required in the group replacement policy.

The problem for such items, then, is to establish a group replacement policy which minimizes the sum of the costs of the items, failures and the replacement operations.

The simplest group replacement policy is one which replaces all items at designated intervals and individually replaces items that fail in between. But more complicated policies are possible. For example, the length of the period between group replacements may be made to depend on the rate of failures in the last group; or items that have been put into service within a certain time before group replacement and which have not failed, may be left in place. Furthermore, items which were removed in operating condition during group replacement, may be ordered by age and used for individual replacements between group replacements. This latter policy is used for replacing expensive street lamps in some cities.

As in the first type of replacement problem a number of techniques are available for handling such problems, both by analysis and simulation. An essential input to these techniques is knowledge of the distribution of times to failure of the items involved. Mathematical statisticians have made available many effective procedures for estimating these distributions.

In both types of replacement problems there are likely to be difficulties in finding the required data. They are seldom maintained on a routine basis.

There is one final type of replacement problem which is growing in importance and which forms a point of contact between the OR scientist and the social psychologist. This is the problem of labor wastage.

The social psychologist will study labor wastage by seeking to assign to every person who leaves a company a quantitative description of his history, together with a qualitative expression of his reasons for leaving. These methods obviously have great power in deriving patterns of behavior.

The approach of the OR worker to this problem tends to be demographic. He will seek to derive a model which expresses the average behavior of a group rather than of an individual. In many cases, he will find that the length of stay of people in a particular company has a well defined pattern. There will be similar relationships for the age at which people change their jobs; marriage is often a prime reason for job changing and hence marriageable age tends to be a peak age for job changing. The degree of skill which workers have obtained will be a factor which the OR scientist will put into his model. The distance people travel to work and the extent of any family ties (brothers or fathers working in the same plant) will also be inserted in the model. There will also be self-aggravating effects; for example, a person leaving a company is more likely to cause other people to leave simply by the unrest his departure causes.

Where such models as these have been found to be very useful is in deciding on the number of people who have to be recruited in order to increase the total number of staff by a given amount. This is one field where OR groups have done OR on themselves, and one large British industrial OR group has shown that if it wishes to increase its strength in the long run by ten people, it will be necessary for it to recruit as many as forty.

Other studies in this field have shown the likely manpower available if a factory is located in a given spot. The models which have been developed in this field are quite interesting in their physical analogies. For example, the chance of retaining a man at a plant can be shown to be proportional to the desirability of the plant, proportional also to the local level of unemployment and approximately inversely proportional to the square of the distance from his home to the plant. In other words, a man behaves as if he were an iron filing under the influence of a magnet where the conductivity of the field is given by the unemployment rate, and the pole strength of the magnet is the intrinsic desirability of the job in question. In this way it is possible to see what is the likely catchment area and labor wastage which would be achieved for a new plant put down in a specific location.

Competitive problems
Now we consider a class of problems in which the decision taken by one decision maker is affected by the decisions made by one or more other decision makers. The relationship between the interacting decision makers may be either cooperative or competitive. As yet, unfortunately, there has been little analysis directed towards increasing the effectiveness of cooperation; but a great deal has been done to increase the effectiveness of competition.

There are many ways of classifying competitive problems, but the following is one of the more useful of these.

1. There are situations in which the competitor's action is known in advance and with certainty; that is, either his actual choice or his method of choice is known without error beforehand. For example, in certain businesses each major competitor usually knows that any reduction of price by him will be met by other major companies.
2. The choice of competition is not known with certainty but can be predicted subject to error. Consequently, there is a risk of being wrong since competition's choices are not known with certainty. For example, in closed competitive bids, on the basis of past history it is possible to determine the likelihood of various bids being placed by specific competitors.
3. Nothing is known in advance about what competition will or is likely to do. Such may be the case in industry with regard to competitive reaction to the introduction of a completely new product. Such ignorance also appears to occur in planning for a future war against an unknown enemy at an unknown time and place.

A second way of classifying competitive situations depends on whether they have a definite termination or continue indefinitely. For example, in bidding for a specific contract there is a definite end to the competitive action. Pricing and advertising of a commodity, on the other hand, may be a relatively continuous competitive process.

Competitive situations may also be classified in terms of the number of competitors involved and whether or not coalitions or mergers can be formed, and whether or not a noncompetitor (e.g. the Government) takes a share of the 'pot'.

The theory of games has provided a conceptual framework within which most competitive problems can be formulated. However, the theory provides solutions of only the simplest types of competitive situations, seldom for ones which actually arise in industry. In most real competitive situations, however, statistical decision theory can be applied successfully.

In situations in which all the alternatives open to competition or the outcome of some of these cannot be explicitly formulated, a type of simulation called *gaming* may be employed. Gaming is a simulation involving real decision makers. That is, the context of the competition is simulated but the decision makers are real.

Military gaming has a long history and is a standard way of training officers and men for combat (competition). But only recently have these techniques been extended to industrial and governmental problems (e.g. in diplomacy) and they have been used as an aid in making decisions in specific situations. We now mention some applications of this technique.

In one case a game was developed which accurately portrayed the major components of a highly competitive market. Managers of the company involved were asked to manage their company in the game as they would normally. The experimenters maintained control over only one variable: the accuracy of the forecasts (provided to the managers) of future demand for the products involved. In this way a determination was made of the payoff that could be associated with increased accuracy of forecasting in the development of competitive strategies.

In another case extensive interviews with managers revealed their concept of how a certain competitive market behaved. The information obtained from these interviews was incorporated into a model which was then converted into a game. The managers were asked to play the game and evaluate the correspondence of the outcome with reality. Their criticism was used to modify the model successively until the game it yielded appeared to behave in the same manner as the actual business did.

Another application of gaming involved the introduction of a new product into the field. Here a research team was created to 'represent' competition and play against the research team representing the sponsor. In this way possible counteractions were explored and evaluated. Plans were prepared for a wider range of eventualities than would otherwise have been anticipated. It also led to considerable modification of the design of the product involved.

It should be noted that the theory of competition can be extended to consider Nature and complex social environments as competitors. This approach can be used, for example, in developing marketing strategies 'against the weather' for products whose sales are greatly affected by it.

Competitive theory has been used effectively in industry to develop bidding tactics, pricing policies, advertising strategies, and timing of the introduction of new models into the market.

Before leaving this type of problem we make one remark. Most managers believe that competitive behavior is not predictable. But in every case involving competition in which we have been involved and of which we have first-hand knowledge, competition was found to have a predictable reaction to most competitive decisions, and more of the kind of data required to make these predictions is generally available than one would guess offhand.

For an interesting and nontechnical introduction to the concepts in the theory of games we suggest the reading of Williams (1954). For a review of gaming and its uses we suggest Cohen and Rhenman (1961).

Search problems
Consider for the moment the problem of searching for submarines in the path of a ship or convoy during time of war. Dirigibles and small airships were used for this purpose. These craft moved slowly over the water at a low altitude and hence had a very high probability of detecting a submarine if it was under them and of not claiming to have detected one when none was there. But because such craft moved slowly they could not 'sweep' a very large area and hence could miss submarines which could come into striking range. If, on the other hand, a very fast plane was used for this purpose, it could cover a much larger area but the accuracy of its observations would be much lower because of its speed and higher altitude. In this case the improved coverage did not compensate for the increased error of observation.

In looking for something, there are two kinds of errors which can be made: (1) failure to detect what one is looking for because of inadequate coverage (*sampling* error), and (2) failure to detect what one is looking for even though one has looked in the right place, or erroneous 'detection' of the thing which is not there (*observational* errors). There are, of course, costs associated with both types of error and with the collection of information.

If one has a fixed amount of resources (time, money, or searchers) a decision must be made as to how much coverage to have (sample size) and what type (sample design). The larger the sample the less is the likelihood of sampling error, but the less time spent per observation, the more likely is an observational error to occur. The selection of an appropriate sample size and design with fixed resources is the *restricted* search problem. In the *unrestricted* version of this type of problem one must also decide how much resources to use in the process. The more resources employed, the greater is the cost of the search but the less is the expected cost of error.

You will probably have recognized by now that auditing is a search procedure and that it raises problems of exactly the type that we have described. Unfortunately, most persons who design auditing procedures are not aware of sampling error and they seem to assume that auditors never make observational errors. Several tests have been carried out to show that this assumption is not justified; that the frequency of auditing errors depends on the amount of time spent with a document and on the individual involved. Using this information it has been possible to design auditing systems for railroads, for example, which consumed less time and money and yield less error than the conventional system that was replaced.

Using search theory a system has been designed for the Railway Express Agency in the United States for allocating revenue obtained from less-than-carload rail shipments which involve several carriers.

Most accounting procedures can be viewed as searches. More generally, all problems of estimation and forecasting are search problems.

Many OR workers have also applied search theory to exploration problems; to determining what areas to explore and how to explore them. In one case involving exploration for nickel it was possible to develop a procedure which reduces the number of holes required to make the necessary estimates by almost 50 per cent. Similar procedures have been applied to prospect for coal.

Search theory is also applicable to the design of inspection procedures and quality control systems. Both types of error, sampling and reservations, are involved and the amounts of money to be spent on inspections must be determined.

There is another type of search problem in which the searching procedure in not under control, but the thing being looked for is under control. For example, most retailers cannot control the search patterns of customers in their store, but they can control the location and allocation of space to goods. This too is a search problem and the same type of theory is applicable to it. It has been used successfully, for example, in placing goods, counters, and departments in supermarkets and department stores.

The critical problem involving the condensation, storage and retrieval of scientific information is also of this type. In what form and how should information be stored so that the costs of retrieving it are minimized? This problem, of course, has not yet been solved, but a good deal of progress has been made.

The techniques which are applicable to the solution of search problems have not been brought together in any one place. It is difficult, therefore, to learn about these techniques. The various components of search theory are discussed in other contexts, such as statistical sampling and estimation theory, and the psychological theory of perception. A brief discussion of a special subset of search problems can be found in Houlden (1961).

Mixed problems
We want to make sure that we do not leave you with the impression that most executive problems fall into *one* of the eight classes which we have just discussed. In fact, neither of us have ever met a problem which falls into only one category. The problems must be analyzed so that these forms can be extracted and the relationship between them can be made explicit. In the airline case discussed in the first chapter, for example, almost every type of problem was involved.

Consider a typical job-shop's production-control problem. First, one must decide how much of each item to make during a planning period (an inventory problem). But it may not be possible to produce the indicated quantitities because they require more machine time than is available. Therefore, either the economic lot sizes must be cut back or production practices altered (an allocation problem). Furthermore, not all the time available on machines may be used because of unexpected delays or breakdowns (a queuing problem) or because a poor sequence has been selected; and so on.

It should also be realized that problems arise which cannot

E

be fitted neatly into any of these categories. From the researcher's point of view these may be the most interesting for they open the possibility of expanding the concepts and techniques employed in OR. Furthermore, there is nothing sacred about the classification which we have used and in fact we are not sure that it is the best. It has changed in the past and will certainly be improved upon in the future. But even in its present form the classification is useful because it enables the manager to perceive what is common among problems and it reminds him that bodies of well-developed techniques are available for solving these problems.

Content of problems

Up to this point we have tried to show that most management problems are reducible to a small number of basic forms, no matter how diverse they are in content. Managers, however, do not normally think of problems in terms of their forms but in terms of their content. Consequently, to give an idea of the range of problems to which OR has been successfully applied in industry we discuss these problems in terms of their content. It would be impossible to provide an exhaustive list of completed studies but we hope that the sample we have selected indicates the type and range of problems that are susceptible to OR.

First we will consider problems which primarily involve only one function of a business and then we will consider some which involve the business as a whole.

Purchasing

OR has been used to develop rules for buying raw materials whose prices are either stable or vary significantly over short periods of time, even day to day. Solutions of this kind of problem involve determining how much to buy when and from whom. Account is taken of storage capacity, deterioration of the material with time or environmental conditions, price, substitutability of materials, location of sources of supply, transportation costs, and so on.

In some cases raw materials are obtained by bidding; for example, in acquiring the rights to drill for oil or metallic deposits. Here it has been necessary to estimate the value of the prospective site, the likelihood of winning for each possible bid, the cost of operations if the bid is won, and to determine on which of the available properties bids should be placed. Perhaps the most striking aspect of these studies is that they demonstrate the predictability of competitive behavior.

OR has also been used to develop strategies for exploring for natural deposits of raw material and to prepare plans for exploiting such resources once they have been located.

A number of studies have been directed at determining whether parts of an assembly should be made or purchased and how this decision should vary depending on plant loading, purchase prices and delivery time.

In the repetitive purchasing of large items of equipment which require stocking spare parts, all aspects of purchasing have been investigated including the effect of nonstandardized equipment on ultimate inventory and repair costs. The question of how many spare parts or whether parts or sub-assemblies should be stocked has also been studied.

In the purchasing of major items of equipment OR has been used to select the type of equipment, and to determine the size that should be acquired, when it should be replaced, and by what. It has also been used to determine when equipment should be rented rather than purchased, and when used or rebuilt equipment is preferable to new.

Production

OR has been used to aid in the design and site selection of plants, to determine how many plants of what size and mix capabilities are required, to what extent they should be automated and how, and what number and type of different kinds of equipment should be installed. It has also been used to design power-generating facilities for a complex of plants, to determine what kinds of power in what quantities are optimal, and how these can best be supplied. It has been employed to determine which plants in a multi-plant operation should be shut down under what conditions, in what order, and how their work should be redistributed among those plants which continue to operate.

OR has frequently been applied to allocating orders for production to that plant which minimizes the sum of production and transportation costs. It has also been used extensively in developing operating policies for plants. These studies have covered such questions as determining production quantities, practices, sequences, and schedules; the nature and location of inventories; what product-mix to produce out of available raw materials; and when shifts should be added or overtime employed. It has also been applied to the design of quality-control systems by developing criteria of acceptability of products through balancing cost and quality, locating inspection activities, and designing the inspection procedures. It has been used to develop maintenance policies, preventive and corrective, and to select between them. It has determined maintenance-crew and facility requirements and how these requirements relate to the policy of equipment replacement and depreciation. OR has also been employed to improve materials handling and internal (as well as external) traffic problems. It has determined how many machines of varying type should be assigned to a single operator so as to get the best balance of material flow and operating costs.

OR has been employed in a variety of studies involving the stabilization of production and employment, and in determining the costs of instability and its impact on the community.

Marketing (*distribution, sales and service*)
OR has been used extensively to determine where distribution points should be located, how large they should be, how much they should stock of what, and whom they should supply.

It has been used to determine how large a sales budget should be and how this budget should be allocated to direct selling, sales promotions, and advertising. The relationship of this allocation to pricing has also been investigated. It has been employed to determine the number of salesmen a company should have, the number and kind of accounts that should be assigned to them, how frequently they should call on each type of account, and what portion of their time should be spent on prospective accounts. The distribution of promotional activity over different accounts has been similarly studied. Advertising expenditures have been optimized for both consumer and industrial products with respect to medium, message and frequency.

OR has been used to determine what kinds of products

consumers need and the variety of sizes, models, colors, and so on that are required. It has been applied to optimizing the timing of new models and to determining in what package and sizes and shapes a product should be marketed.

It has been employed to determine whether service should be provided by the manufacturer or private individuals, what service should be provided and what kind of guarantee for what period should be offered.

It has also been used in locating retail outlets, determining their size and design, allocating their internal space to display and stock, and to determining whether they should be company or privately operated. Franchise and fair trading systems have been evaluated.

Research and development
OR has recently been applied to determining what the budget for research and development should be, how this should be divided between basic and applied or other types of research, and how individual projects should be selected for support. It has been used also to determine what size of research and development facility and staff are required, and how they can be used most effectively. Organization of such activities have also been studied.

OR has been employed to determine the areas in which research and development should be concentrated, in developing criteria for evaluating alternative designs, and in determining how long a life and how much reliability should be designed into a product.

It is being used with increased frequency to schedule and control large scale development projects and for determining the time and cost requirements of such projects.

Sequencing and spotlighting bottlenecks
In many complex operations the total job may be broken down into a large number of elements. Some of these elements have to wait for others to be completed before they can be started. Other sets of elements can be carried out in parallel. Once these linkages and dependencies have been established it is possible to determine that particular sequence of elements which is critical—i.e. which immediately follow each other, for the whole

job to be done in minimum time. Hence the name 'critical path method'.

Often it is possible to reduce the time certain elements will take at the expense of increasing their costs. Critical path will work out the total-cost–minimum-time relationship.

The method has been developed to cases where the time for an element is subject to great uncertainty (Project Evaluation Review Technique or PERT).

These methods are used with great effectiveness in complex planning or construction projects.

Personnel

OR has been used to determine what mix of age and skills among workers is most desirable, what causes accidents and how they can and should be prevented, and what causes absenteeism and labor turnover and how these can be minimized.

It has been employed to establish ways of recruiting personnel, for effectively classifying them, assigning them to jobs, and for measuring their performance in these jobs. It has been used to improve incentive schemes and hence productivity.

Use is being made of OR to determine how the benefits of automation can be fairly distributed over those affected by it and to develop schemes by which automation can be accelerated without undue hardship to anyone involved.

Finance and accounting

OR has been used to design accounting and auditing procedures which minimize the sum of the cost of the procedure and error. It has been employed in developing automated data processing and accounting procedures, for scheduling and controlling the quality of manual accounting, and, in general, to control office operations. It has been used extensively in the development of sampling procedures for accounting to provide information of required accuracy more quickly than would otherwise be available for management. Sampling has also been employed in developing optimal routines for dealing with claims and complaints.

Credit policies for a company have been studied and procedures for estimating credit risks and processing delinquents have been developed.

OR has been used in determining long-range capital requirements and how to generate these requirements. It has also been applied to the design of investment portfolios and for maintaining these under changing conditions.

Overall planning
A number of overall planning projects have been undertaken in which OR has played a central role. Such plans have covered specifications of objectives for the business as a whole and for each part of it for each of a series of years. Programs for generating and developing resources (men, machines, material and money) have been prepared and allocations of these to functions have been analyzed. The plans have also included determination of optimal operating policies, organizational structure, and internal communication systems.

OR has also been employed to develop long-range plans for product diversification and development; that is, for changing the nature of the business. It has been employed to prepare for the merger of companies which provide overlapping services and competing goods by planning the transition as well as the ultimate working arrangements.

Conclusion
It will be apparent to the manager that in the previous account few problems have been mentioned which have not, at some time or another, been investigated by some type of research other than OR. This fact underlines the important point we have tried to make, namely that OR is *not* distinguished by what it investigates, but by *how* it conducts its investigations. If one does want to distinguish OR by the problems with which it deals, he would do much better to concern himself with the problem-complexes or problems with which an OR study terminates rather than with the (frequently) simple problems with which it begins. It should be remembered that the problem as management sees it may not be a problem, but a set of symptoms as the OR worker sees it. The diagnostic process may be an involved and complex one in which the overall ramifications of the symptoms to the overall system must be thoroughly explored.

3 Relationship with other Management Services

FOR MANY, many years the long-suffering OR worker has had to face standard questions which are asked at the end of every talk which he gives on OR. One which comes up time and time again is: 'What is the difference between OR and method study?' or: 'What is the difference between OR and industrial engineering?' and so on. Managers and executives are constantly being importuned by the pleading cries of the scientist or management consultant to pay attention to this or that specialty or new technique. It is difficult for the industrialist not to become confused; it is difficult for him to be able to regard all these separate disciplines in perspective and to be able to sort out the meretricious from the intrinsically valuable.

Fortunately, there are the three characteristics discussed in the first chapter (the open-system approach, inter disciplinary teams, and a methodology based on the use of mathematical models) by which one can always judge whether a solution to a problem has been obtained by OR.

What is this touchstone, this guiding point which determines whether or not OR is being carried out? It is, as we have shown in Chapter 2, the concept of the model. OR is the study of complex systems of men, machines, money and materials, and the systems are studied by deriving a mathematical or analogical model which expresses the performance of the system in question. If any operation is studied in this way and a model is produced, then we have an operations research study. If this is not done, then we may be in the realms of industrial engineering or method study or accountancy or ergonomics, but we will certainly not be in the realms of OR.

Nevertheless, it is not sufficient to erect an ivory tower, to place OR within it like a virtuous maiden and then seek to keep all the lusty young knights of other specialties at a respectable distance. The maiden and the knights must mix in a dialectical process. If we deny full intercourse between the management disciplines we shall find that we have a sterile situation.

It is the claim of the OR worker that he studies organized man, machine, material, money systems, that leads some workers in other management specialties to complain that the OR worker has a Messianic complex. There is the feeling that the OR man has a god-like view, that he studies the complete problem and everyone else is inferior. This is not so, and it is unfortunate that some OR workers have allowed this impression to grow. For a specialist in any of the separate management disciplines to work effectively he must be prepared to raise his eyes from his particular specialty and to study the whole picture. This is the moment at which he comes into contact with and works alongside the OR worker.

If we are, then, to state the relative fields of activity of all these management specialists, we have to look at the whole company or industrial activity as defined and described through our concept of the system. As has been stated above, we are considering and studying *organized* man, machine, material, money systems. For a set of activities and entities to be regarded as an organized system four distinct criteria must be satisfied. These are that the system must have content, structure, communication and control. By these, we mean the following.

1. *Content*—Men and machines are among the entities making up the system. Furthermore, we find that most such systems are engaged in converting one set of resources (inputs, such as material and money) into another more valued type of resource (outputs, such as goods or services). Such a system, then, usually contains four types of things: men, machines, material and money.

2. *Structure*—The activity of the system is divided functionally and different parts of the system are responsible for different subactivities. That is, there is a functional division of labor; not all the components of the system are doing the same thing, but most (or a significant portion) of what they do is intended to serve some overall objectives of the system.

3. *Communication*—The human elements of the system must be capable of responding to each other's activities and to the behavior of the system's environment either as the result of direct observation or by receipt of relevant information from those who have observed it. Hence, communication holds the parts of the system together and keeps it in contact with its environment.

4. *Control*—The system must be capable of evaluating its own performance relative to its objectives and of changing itself so as to improve its performance. Therefore, it must be capable of modifying its own content, structure, communications, and even controls in order better to approximate its objectives. In short, the system must be *adaptive* and *self-organizing*.

Let us now take these four aspects of the system in turn and see how far the different management specialties which are available play their part in improving the performance of the various parts of the system.

The first item is that of content and, as has been stated already, this consists of four components, men, machines, materials and money.

Content

When we study the use of men in a system we have three main avenues of approach. We can, first of all, study the selection and training of the men, that is a study of the input of this particular part of the content of the system. Improving the input can be done either by making a better selection initially or by improving those already available through training or, of course, by both of these approaches. This approach is that of the personnel psychologist who, in effect, takes all aspects of an organization other than its men as fixed and looks on the personnel as the controllable variable. In recent years there has been a tremendous development of management and supervisory training programs. It has now been recognized that it is through improving individuals in a system and by devoting care and attention to them that a company can grow, for it is the individual, his latent skills and talents, which are the unseen assets which do not appear on the balance sheet of a company and which in the end dominate its performance. In addition, a great deal of time and money is now being spent on personnel selection procedures, and there are now emerging a number of specialist companies which offer advice in this particular field.

Having got our personnel, another way of effecting an improvement is to improve their behavior. In this, we take the operations which have to be performed by the people and we try to improve their performance in this situation. This is the approach taken in time and motion or work studies and is usually associated with industrial engineering.

The third avenue of approach to the problem of assisting the improvement in the performance of men is by changing the work environment. Efforts are made to improve the performance of men by modifying their physical, psychological and social environment. Man's behavior is controlled indirectly by changing such aspects of his environment as incentives, fringe benefits, status relationships, management and worker attitudes towards each other and recreational facilities. The famous Hawthorne studies typify this approach which is associated with industrial psychology and social psychology.

The second component part of a system is the machines. We may take this particular problem in two parts. There is, first of all, the design, construction and maintenance of individual pieces of equipment, and there is secondly the integration of these pieces of equipment together into an engineering system. The design, construction and maintenance of individual pieces of equipment intended for a particular job are the concern of the traditional and classical branches of engineering such as mechanical, chemical, civil and electrical engineering. The traditional approach that all these fields make is to attempt to obtain the best equipment system by joining together individually designed pieces of equipment, each of which is considered to be best in terms of its own restricted function. This procedure is likely to lead to serious error and we shall cover some points on this later. This first approach might be loosely called fitting the equipment to the job. The next task is to fit the equipment to the operator. In this area we find many pieces of equipment fail because, for them to be operated efficiently in practice, unrealistic and unreasonable demands are made on the human operators.

Considerations of human factors in the design of equipment has come to be known as human engineering or ergonomics.

In this particular field, as in traditional engineering, we take the machine as the variable which can be controlled, but the emphasis on the factors which should be taken into account in design is quite different. Ergonomicists, or human engineers, are more likely to be psychologists with an interest in engineering than engineers with an interest in psychology. Consequently, they do not take complete responsibility for the design of equipment. They work with design engineers and in so doing, by this interaction, they lead to more consideration being given to human factors, and hence an improvement in performance of the man and the machine taken together as a team can be derived.

Finally, there is the integration of successive pieces of equipment together to form a system. Systems engineering is a natural extension of work which was done many years ago on plant layout by industrial engineers. It is, however, more highly developed than these early studies. It makes more use of mathematical analysis and concerns itself primarily with electronic controls. It is, in effect, a child of the second industrial revolution.

The third component of the system is the materials which are used. Studies in this field will naturally bring in the metallurgists and the chemical engineers, the civil engineers and the quality-control statisticians, the chemist and the physicist. All these specialists will take the influence of the material on the working of the whole system and will seek to concern themselves with this one type of variable.

Finally, and of major importance, is the flow of money through an industrial system. The generation of the information necessary to do this is the task of accounting, and the evaluation of this flow is normally a comptroller's function. It is a welcome development in recent years that accountants are beginning to cease restricting their attention to the derivation of information and extending their view to that of the use to which the information is put. Industrial economists have turned more and more to mathematical analysis and hence their approach has a great deal in common, from the technological point of view, with systems engineering and OR.

Structure

The study of organizational structure has not reached the maturity and sophistication of studies of organizational content. Only in the last decade has a quantitative theory of organization begun to emerge (see Haire, 1959). As yet, this theory is difficult to apply in the real world. Consequently, practical studies of organizational structure (e.g. company reorganizational studies) are still largely judgmental and qualitative in character. They rely more on experience than experiment. No particular discipline specializes in such studies; they are normally done by traditional management consultants.

There is an increasing number of efforts to study organizational structure scientifically. Within the next decade such studies will surely become commonplace.

Communication

Study of this aspect of organization is in much the same state as that of structure. Although there is a highly developed mathematical theory of communication (Shannon and Weaver, 1949), it is only relevant to the purely engineering aspects of communication systems; that is, to the design and operation of physical components. It has little or no relevance to the psychological and sociological aspects of communication. It does not deal with the meaning of the messages transmitted. There is, however, an emerging theory of human communication (Cherry, 1958; Ackoff, 1958) but as yet it has found relatively little application.

Practical studies of communication systems in an organization are therefore largely judgmental and qualitative in character. They are performed primarily by *systems and procedures or organization and methods analysts*. Because of the growing role of electronic computers and other related electronic devices in communication systems, more and more use is being made by these analysts of mathematical and electronic concepts (particularly network theory) in the design of that kind of communication system devoted to integrated data processing.

Control

This approach to organizational problems concentrates on the process by which an organization's management directs it towards its objectives. This process has two aspects: (1) detection of deviations of performance from an acceptable standard or detection of changes in conditions which will result in a significant loss of effectiveness, and (2) adjusting the behavior of the organization so as to improve its performance. These two phases of control, it will be observed, are equivalent to formulating and solving a problem: perceiving the need for a decision and making it.

Such decisions involve the selection and utilization of resources (men, machines, material and money) an organizational structure, a communication system, and a control process itself. The emphasis, however, is not on the content of the decision, but on its structure: the way it is arrived at. This approach is taken by OR.

Although content, structure and communications are all involved in control, they are not in themselves the subject of inquiry in OR. The decisions by which they are selected, designed and utilized are the subject of study. OR must utilize the subject knowledge supplied by specialists in organizational content, structure, and communications in order to accomplish control. Furthermore, these specialists can operate most effectively when supplied with the kinds of operating specifications which OR can supply.

To illustrate the relationship of OR to other disciplines we might take some work which was carried out in the British coal industry a few years ago. The British coal industry, as part of its development program, drives approximately 100 miles of tunnel each year and they were at this time involved in a 10-year program for tunnel drivage: that is, 1,000 miles of tunnel to be driven in a 10-year program. By any manner of means, this is quite a respectable task to set oneself. Since these tunnels were aimed at exploiting new areas of coal, it was of vital importance that they be driven as quickly as possible. Many studies were carried out on tunnelling performance. The method study engineer was able to relate the deployment of men and machines to best advantage. The geologists and the explosive engineers were studying the relationship between the pattern of holes drilled in the face of the rock prior to explosion with the distribution of the size of the rubble which resulted, and this distribution was used in designing adequate and efficient machinery for moving away the pile of debris after the explosion. The research scientists were studying the development of new forms of explosives which would work to better advantage in the restricted confines of a tunnel face. All these specialists were working as part of an effort to increase tunnelling speeds. When the OR team was invited to play their part in this particular investigation many people wondered what extra value this team would be able to supply. The OR team studied tunnelling operations in a large number of locations and as a result were able to derive a model which showed the relationship between tunnelling speed and the number of men employed in the team, the number of holes which they drilled in the rock face, the type of loading equipment which was employed for shifting away the debris and all the other many factors which could be taken into account in this sort of operation. There were, in fact, dozens of factors which could be assumed to be important and many of these factors were the subject of research and development effort.

When the model was examined closely it was seen that there were only three factors which paid any major part in determining tunnelling speed. These were the factors for which, from an examination of the model, it could be seen that a small improvement would give a major improvement in tunnelling speed. These three factors were the degree of organization of the tunnelling team, the rate at which the debris could be loaded and taken away and the total length of holes which had to be drilled in the face of the rock. Hence, research could now be channelled into three specific operations. There was the use of method study for improving the organization and efficiency of a team. There was the correct selection of equipment for loading away the debris (there was no question here of having to design special equipment, the correct equipment existed but it was not being used in the appropriate places) and finally, the research physicists were given the task of developing explosives which would be such that the total length of holes to be drilled would be minimal. The model could achieve one further important result. It could state the amount of money which it was worth investing on each of these three lines of improvement, in order for the return on the expenditure to be worthwhile. In any industry this is often a point which is a matter of speculation. But here it was possible, by means of the model, to look at the research and development program in terms of the return on an investment.

The point here is that OR does not replace the need for any of the more specialized disciplines and approaches to management's problems, but it does provide a basis for integrating their efforts and for determining when they can most effectively be used.

It must be apparent that the classification of approaches to organizational problems just given is not as clean-cut as one might hope. There is an increasing amount of borrowing of techniques and points of view between these approaches. (It is for this reason that this complex has come to be known generally as 'the Management Sciences'.) The diversity of offerings makes it necessary for a manager who seeks aid to decide what brand is best suited to his situation. It has become more and more difficult to do this. The proliferation of management services seems to have created a need for specialists who can determine which scientific or engineering service should be used in a particular problem situation. But it has not come to this extreme because the various specialties are becoming increasingly well informed about each other and are frequently being combined in management research units. Through collaboration a group of specialists can determine in an initial analysis of a problem what one or combination of approaches is likely to be most fruitful.

The moral of this discussion then is that there is a growing need for an executive function with responsibility for coordinating management research services; one that integrates them so as to produce the best performance of these services (and hence of the organization) as a whole.

A manager who devotes his time to the matter can come to understand the potentialities and limitation of each type of service to the company without himself being able to provide any of them. Such understanding can assure the company that its management is as advanced technologically as are its production processes.

4 Organization
and Administration

IN THIS chapter we deal with the questions which are most likely to be asked by managers. We hope that these questions will cover most of those that are likely to have arisen in the reader's mind regarding the way in which OR can be started and get operating quickly and effectively in a company.

In answering some of the questions it will be necessary, if the answer is to be of any value, to name persons and organizations. In doing this two risks are run, we may omit some people and organizations which should be included and, alternatively, we may include some people and organizations which should really be omitted. We make no pretence at completeness of the lists provided and we want to emphasize that inclusion in any listing in this chapter does not necessarily constitute approval or endorsement of the person or organization involved.

How to start

First we will consider how a company can get started in OR. In order to begin, a research team is needed and this can be made up in three ways: (1) externally, by hiring a consulting group, (2) internally, by recruiting experienced OR men or training men already in the organization, and (3) by some combination of these.

Before discussing these possibilities we express our strong belief that the ultimate place of OR should be within the company. This does not mean that outside groups may not be useful either initially or in the long run, but rather that every company involved in OR should aim to have its own OR group. Our discussion of the three alternatives is based upon and biased by this point of view.

F

Starting with external help

It may be that you have an urgent problem, the solution of which you want as quickly as possible. In this case, the best thing you can do is to engage an experienced outside organization to perform the necessary research. This is by far the quickest way to get an initial problem solved. Such a start, however, has some disadvantages. In the first place it does not leave the company with any greater internal capability of doing OR than it had before the first investigation was started. In addition, it leaves the company with no capability of adapting the solution obtained to changing conditions. This second point can, of course, be quite important since business is carried out in a dynamic environment and conditions are constantly changing.

In the light of this, we strongly urge that at least one technically competent man in the company be assigned to work closely with any outside agency that is employed to do OR. This means, of course, that we are now involved in the third alternative, namely, using both internal and external help. Since we regard this alternative as being so important, we will consider in more detail what is involved in it. Before doing so, a list of *some* of the sources of outside help in OR may be useful.

As we shall discuss the existence of criteria for OR competence later in the chapter, we merely list now those groups which have on their staff full members of the Operations Research Society of America and the Operational Research Society (United Kingdom). *This list does not necessarily mean that any group not included is incompetent, neither does it mean necessarily that all those included have our seal of approval.* Our list is precisely and no more than that which we state, namely, and we repeat, that these groups contain scientists who are recognized by the Operations Research Societies of the United States and the United Kingdom as being in their view competent OR workers.

UNITED STATES OF AMERICA

Consultants

Analytical Associates, New York
Arthur Andersen & Co., New York
Arthur D. Little, Inc., Cambridge, Mass
Arthur Young & Co., New York

UNITED STATES OF AMERICA

Consultants (cont.)
Broadview Research Corp.
Booz, Allen & Hamilton, Chicago
Booz Allen Applied Res., Bethesda, Md.
Council for Economic & Industrial Research, Inc., Arlington, Va.
Dunlap & Assoc., Stamford, Conn.
Ernst & Ernst, Cleveland
Fair, Isaac & Co., San Francisco
John Diebold & Assoc., Philadelphia
Lybrand, Ross Bros. & Montgomery, New York
McKinsey & Co., New York
Martin K. Starr Assoc., New York
Mathematica Inc., Princeton, N.J.
National Analysts, Philadelphia
Operations Research, Inc., Silver Springs, Md.
Peat, Marwick, Caywood, Schiller & Co., Chicago
Price Waterhouse & Co., New York
Stillson Assoc., Panorama City, Calif.
Technical Operations, Inc., Burlington, Mass.
Touche, Ross, Bailey & Smart, New York

Academic Institutions and Research Institutes
Armour Research Foundation, Chicago
Batelle Memorial Institute, Columbus, Ohio
Carnegie Institute of Technology, Pittsburgh
Case Institute of Technology, Cleveland
Cornell University, Ithaca, N.Y.
Massachusetts Institute of Technology, Cambridge, Mass.
Midwest Research Institute, Kansas City
New York University, New York
Northwestern University, Evanston, Ill.
Ohio State University, Columbus, Ohio
Purdue University, Lafayette, Ind.
Stanford Research Institute, Menlo Park, Calif.
The John Hopkins University, Baltimore, Md.
The Research Triangle Institute, Durham, N.C.
The University of Michigan, Ann Arbor, Mich.
The University of North Carolina, Chapel Hill, N.C.

UNITED KINGDOM

Consultants
Arthur Andersen & Co., London
Associated Industrial Consultants, London

UNITED KINGDOM

Consultants (Cont.)
  Business Operations Research, London
  C.E.I.R. Ltd., London
  ORbit (Operational Analysis and Research) Ltd.
  K. Pennycuick, Limited, Biggleswade, Beds.
  Science in General Management (SIGMA) Ltd., Croydon, Surrey
  Touche, Ross, Bailey & Smart Limited, London
  Urwick, Orr & Partners, London

Academic Institutions
  Imperial College, London
  London School of Economics
  Manchester College of Science & Technology
  University of Birmingham

In selecting an outside organization to give assistance in OR there are several things which should be done. First you should discuss your problem with a number of consulting groups so that you have a basis of comparison. Second, you should obtain a list of previous clients of each group's research efforts, and discuss their performance with the firms who have used them. Finally you should determine how willing the groups are to have internal company personnel work with them on problems.

Starting with internal help
Let us be quite clear, it would be a mistake, if not a disaster, to begin internal company OR without one experienced and qualified OR worker. This man may be supplemented by inexperienced (in OR) scientists or engineers who will be trained in the process of working on problems. Recruiting a competent OR man is a great problem since the demand exceeds the supply. Salaries for good OR men are high and it takes time, maybe up to a year to find one. The economics of the market place apply here and, within general limits, you will get what you pay for.

United States—An OR man with sufficient experience to direct an OR activity cannot be obtained for less than $15,000 per year, but salaries between $18,000 and $25,000 are more common. Some top people in the field may cost even more.

Recent Ph.D.s in OR who have some industrial experience cost about $15,000 per year. Many are quite capable of running a small OR activity. Hence, universities offering this degree (a list is provided later) are a source of men, but the national output is quite small (on the order of 20 to 25 per year). These men should be contacted in the fall before their graduation. Last year the OR graduates at one institution had an average of 21 offers each and most made their job selections quite early in the academic year.

Advertisements in the journals *Operations Research* and *Management Science* will reach the experienced personnel in the field and are quite inexpensive. Ads may be placed with the following:

Operations Research: Charles P. Chadsey, Advertising Manager, Research Analysis Corporation, 6935 Arlington Road, Bethesda 14, Md.

Management Science: Harold H. Cauvet, Business Manager, P.O. Box 273, Pleasantville, New York.

Establishing an internal OR group commits management. An intervening non-committing stage may be desirable in some cases, and this can be achieved by forming a temporary task force with a limited life of six months or a year. If organizational changes later become desirable, these can be made without embarrassment to anyone.

Evaluating applicants may be a problem. It is best to solicit opinions of competent OR men and to consult the membership list of the Operations Research Society of America. A person who is a member, in contrast to an associate member, in not necessarily competent; but most competent practitioners are members. OR men in nearby academic institutions can usually help you in evaluating applicants.

United Kingdom—An OR man with sufficient experience to direct competently an OR activity cannot be obtained for much less than £3,000 a year, and salaries between £3,000 and £4,000 a year are becoming more common. The top people in OR will, of course, cost even more.

There has been in recent years a trickle of OR men who not only have post-graduate industrial experience but also post-graduate degrees in operational research. To take an example, a man who graduated with a good class honors degree in science or mathematics or engineering, who has worked in industry for perhaps 3 years and has then gone back to university to do a 1 year M.Sc. course in operational research, would command a salary of about £1,800 a year. Universities offering Masters and Doctorates in Operational Research are a source of recruitment but the national output is quite small, at present it is of the order of about 6 people a year. If you wish to contact one of these men you should approach universities in December of each year for a man who is likely to qualify in the following summer.

Advertisements in the usual Sunday newspapers will contact most OR personnel, but perhaps the best field for advertising is in the *Quarterly Operational Research*. Advertisements in this journal are quite inexpensive and will reach every qualified OR man in the country. Advertisements may be placed with the Pergamon Press, Headington Hill Hall, Oxford.

Selecting a short list from the applicants to an advertisement and making the final choice of the man who will lead your activity is difficult, especially if you have no experience in the OR field. If you require help in this particular problem we suggest that you solicit the opinions of the leading OR men in the country, who may be contacted via the Operational Research Society, 64 Cannon Street, London, E.C.4. Alternatively, you may refer to the membership list of the Society and consult any full members with whom you may be acquainted, or approach nearby academic institutions to help you evaluate the applicants.

Internal recruitment

An alternative to recruiting an experienced OR man is to appoint someone from inside the company. If you do this, he must of necessity be a highly competent scientist or engineer and you must give him sufficient time and resources to train himself. You must give him at least a year in which to soak himself in the literature of the subject and to spend some time visiting well established industrial OR groups. If you approach the problem in a tactful fashion it is quite possible that one of the larger OR groups in industry or at a university would be willing to take on your man and let him work within their group in order to give him experience. If you have a potentially good man, then this offer by an outside group will not be as generous as it seems, since they will be able to use him profitably on their own investigational work. At the end of a year your man could begin his first project with the occasional help of an outside consultant.

In selecting men from within a company there are a number of factors which should be considered.

1. At least two men should be selected. Experience has shown that activities that begin with one man are less likely to develop and expand than those which start with two or more. It is important to remember that an OR man working on his own in a company is denied the opportunity of sparking off his ideas in conversation with a fellow creature who is interested in his own speciality. To deny him this contact is to invite him to wither and die. In addition, the interdisciplinary approach requires at least two men.

2. At least one of the men selected should know the company in its full breadth. He should know the people involved in each function of the business so that it is easy for him to approach key people in each function.

3. Each person initially selected must have a good degree in mathematics, engineering or science. In addition, each one selected, regardless of background should have a good command of mathematical thinking. They should have a knowledge of elementary statistics and probability theory. If they have not got this basic requirement then, during part of their 12-months' training period, they should be asked to obtain a grasp of these subjects as rapidly as possible. If they find it difficult to get a working knowledge of statistics and probability in this time then they are not right for OR anyway and should be moved back into their own specialities.

4. They should like to work on real live problems and not be over-attracted to a purely theoretical approach.

5. They should be interested in coping with complexity and not try to simplify complex systems out of existence.

6. This particular point stems from the preceding one, namely that they should appreciate the primacy of the problem rather than of the technique. The task of OR is to develop techniques for existing problems. The task is not, repeat *not*, to search for problems to fit existing techniques.

7. They must be articulate and be able to use the language of management and operating personnel alike. They must be prepared to be misunderstood and they must be prepared to accept the real world as it is. They should want to have others understand what they are doing and not merely accept it. Beware of scientists who are intellectual snobs, who feel superior because of their training, experience, degree or alma mater.

8. The two men selected should supplement each other, not only in background, but in temperament. It is, for example, very useful if one of them has his main interest in the analysis of problems and the other mainly interested in data collection and manipulation.

Joint efforts

In our opinion, the most effective way of starting in OR involves using an outside agency in combination with personnel from within the company. The problem can then be assigned to the joint group and the company men can be trained in the course of doing the research. The training should not be restricted to that obtained by working together. Arrangements must be made for regularly scheduled classes or seminars in which OR is systematically studied by company personnel under the supervision of an experienced OR man. There should also be arrangements made for the personnel to attend some of the short courses which are now being run in various parts of the United States and United Kingdom. A list of these courses appears later in this chapter.

If the men selected from within the company are capable and of the right education, then by the end of a year they can begin to share technical responsibility for the OR and by the end of the second year they should be able to proceed with only occasional outside consultation.

Notwithstanding that after 2 years your personnel should be well able to deal with the majority of the OR work with which they are likely to be faced, there are some advantages in the continued use of an outside group even after this period. First there is the assurance of continued objectivity. It is easy for internal personnel to acquire the preconceptions or misconceptions of managerial personnel in the company and hence to be inclined to try to prove or disprove certain points, depending on the team's attitude to the manager involved. Second, it is frequently easier for an outsider to get access to certain information and to obtain access to senior management than for an insider. For these reasons, many companies who have highly sophisticated and well established internal OR groups retain the services of an outside research organization on a consulting basis.

Mixture of team

An industrial OR problem seldom arises which requires more than five or six men to work on it. In developing a group which will work simultaneously on several problems it is reasonable to plan on an average of three men per project, and certainly not less than two. One researcher may work on more than one problem at a time, but each man should have a primary assignment to one particular problem.

If we were going to build up an OR team from men inexperienced in OR and could get people from whatever disciplines we desired, we think we would 'acquire disciplines' in the following order:

1 and 2. A physical scientist and an engineer.

It is curious that in general physicists make better OR workers than chemists. In the U.S.A. mechanical, electrical and chemical engineers have good backgrounds for OR. In the U.K. it is very difficult to persuade engineers to leave their specialities, in which they are very highly paid, and to move into an unchartered region.

3. A mathematician or a statistician.

4. A biologist. The advantage of biology is that it deals with the uncontrolled situation in which it is not possible very easily to carry out controlled statistical experiments.

5. A mathematical economist.

6. A behavioral scientist.

7. A cost analyst.

In general, a good division of an OR group would be roughly one-third physical scientists and engineers, one-third mathematicians and statisticians and one-third biologists, behavioral scientists and economists.

Training company men

We have already mentioned that an experienced man can guide the training of technical personnel drawn from within a company. This task is made easier by the number of text books that are available on the techniques employed in OR. Internal courses should be organized along academic lines as much as possible by being regularly scheduled, involving reading and discussion and working of examples which should be subjected to a critical evaluation by the outside OR man.

Many universities, institutes of technology and technical colleges now run courses in OR. These can be used in place of internal classes. The courses are of various types and range from the short courses of perhaps two-weeks' duration, up to the full-time degree courses at master or doctorate level.

The list of organizations and institutions which run OR courses is rather long and is constantly changing. Consequently, we suggest that if you require up-to-date information on current courses in operations research of various types you should contact the Operations Research Society of America or the Operational Research Society (United Kingdom). The following is a list of academic institutions offering various types of OR courses:

UNITED STATES

Short courses
    Carnegie Institute of Technology
    Case Institute of Technology
    Cornell University
    Johns Hopkins University
    Massachusetts Institute of Technology
    Ohio State University
    Purdue University
    University of Michigan
    University of California, Los Angeles
    University of California, Berkeley

Graduate work
    Carnegie Institute of Technology
    Case Institute of Technology
    Clarkson College of Technology
    Columbia University

UNITED STATES

Graduate work (cont.)
  Cornell University
  George Washington University
  Harvard University
  Johns Hopkins University
  Massachusetts Institute of Technology
  Northwestern University
  Ohio State University
  Oklahoma State University
  Purdue University
  Stanford University
  University of Arizona
  University of California, Berkeley
  University of California, Los Angeles
  University of Chicago
  University of Michigan
  University of North Carolina
  University of Pennsylvania
  Wayne State University
  Yale University

UNITED KINGDOM

Short courses
  University of Birmingham
  London School of Economics
  Manchester College of Science and Technology
  University of Durham
  Northampton College of Advanced Technology
  Royal Technical College, Glasgow
  College of Aeronautics, Cranfield

Post graduate courses
  University of Birmingham (Degree)
  London School of Economics (Diploma)
  Imperial College, London (Diploma)
  Manchester College of Science and Technology (Degree)
  Cardiff Technical College (Diploma)
  College of Aeronautics, Cranfield (Diploma)
  University of Hull (Diploma)

In addition there are the regular meetings of the Operations Research Society of America and of the Operational Research Society. These are particularly useful for learning who is working on what problem and for identifying sources of relevant information on the various types of problems which might arise. Information regarding these meetings can be obtained from the two Societies, from which information may also be obtained regarding periodicals and journals in this field.

Location of OR in a company

This subject has received a great deal of attention but unfortunately most of the discussion is based on the false assumption that there is a *best* location for OR. This is not so. In considering where to locate in a company we must first of all balance certain factors and must also see whether some factors do not of themselves mean that certain parts of the organization would definitely be wrong for the OR activity.

One of the greatest potential uses of OR in a company is at the top strategy-making level. Consequently, the OR man *must* have access to the directors (top managers) of the company concerned. This does not necessarily mean that he should report immediately to the director, or vice-president but the line of access must be there. To do anything else is to deny yourself the full dividends coming from using OR in your company. This may mean that you make your OR man report to the heads of one of your departments. You may, for example, let him report directly to the head of production. Alternatively, he may report to the head of finance. The advantage of such a setting in the company structure is that it gives a firm basis for the OR activity. It is well rooted in the structure of the company, it is forced into the front line of decision making and hence its work will have an immediate usefulness. Finally, it is not subject to sudden change in the atmosphere in which its work is carried out if there is a change in the company personnel. The disadvantage of such a location is the obvious one, namely, that an OR team located in a production department will work mainly on production problems and may ultimately come to be regarded as the production department's advocates. A second alternative is to locate the OR group within the company's research department. This puts the OR worker among his fellow scientists and he works in a pleasant atmosphere of scientific objectivity.

Unfortunately, it also divorces them from the main stream of decision-making within the company and, of course, in many companies the research department is a back-room activity which is carried on without much regard for either the clock or even the calendar. Such an atmosphere can be disastrous for OR and you should think very carefully if you are going to put OR in the pure or applied research department of your company.

A final alternative which is sometimes adopted is to incorporate OR in one of the other management specialities (such as industrial engineering or work method study or in systems and procedures or organization and methods groups). We feel quite strongly that such a placement is to put the kiss of death on the OR activity. In exactly the same way an OR group which had an industrial engineering or method study group incorporated within it might do very good OR, but its work study activity would probably be of poor quality and of low usefulness. These specialities are all important and if they are going to exist in contact with each other they must exist side by side on equal status. This leads to the setting up in some companies of management services groups. There is much to commend this and we suggest that you give this very serious consideration. The danger of a management service group is that it can get divorced from the main activity and it can be staffed by managers who have failed in routine line management. Such people do not carry the respect of the line managers and consequently an OR group or any other specialist group located in such a management services activity can be under a grave stigma from the start.

When all is said and done, the placing of an OR group in an organization is largely a matter of common sense. Organizations consist of groups of people communicating with and controlling each other. The OR man must report to someone who is sympathetic to what he is trying to do. He must be so securely located that if this man moves on elsewhere he will not find himself out on a limb. He must have access to the top management of the company and he must have ready access to all the information of the company. If all these conditions are achieved then it matters little in what particular branch he is formally located, for his parish will be the company and not his particular department.

The problems on which to start

The importance of the first problem which an OR team tackles cannot be underestimated. This is the shop window. When the team starts work, most of the management in the company will know that they are moving into operation and most of the management of the company will have no real idea at all of what it is they are trying to do, why they are trying to do it, how they are going to do it, nor what is likely to be achieved if they are successful. In the first stages of an OR group's activity it is quite usual for the problems they are asked to tackle to be based on the technology of the processes of the company concerned. It may be that their work will have a very large technological content and this, although it may deny the OR worker the full possibility of displaying all the techniques at his disposal, will be an advantage since the manager who goes through the final report will find that it is written in the language of his own speciality. As time goes on, the OR worker will gradually move away from the technologically-based studies and will be able to develop into the classical realms of OR. Hence the first job is likely to be in the general area of production. Other advantages stemming from this are that production managers are accustomed to looking at their problems in a quantitative fashion, and to have outsiders come in to look over their shoulder and advise them on what they should be doing. This has a disadvantage in that a lot of the cream has already been skimmed off the milk. Consequently, the savings from an OR study on production processes are unlikely to be high. As time goes on the OR team will be able to direct the attention of the management to problems which the members think important, and will also be able to draw the attention of management to successfully completed studies in these particular areas which have been carried out elsewhere. The knowledge that a competitor has successfully carried out OR in a particular field of the company's activity is the greatest stimulus to a company carrying out OR within that particular field themselves.

A danger which management must guard against is the conversion of the OR effort into one that is used to 'put out fires'. There will be a temptation to use a good team in this way. OR men generally develop that kind of knowledge of operations which is very useful in emergency situations. Although some fire-fighting activity by OR men is desirable, only a small amount of their total effort should be spent in this way. The major contribution which OR can make involves problems of wide scope and long range; problems which, if solved, prevent crises in the future. Prevention of future crises cannot be accomplished by a team that is preoccupied with current crises.

Time and cost

In general, industrial OR projects seem to take between 3 and 12 months to complete. A new OR team of two or three people should, after its initial birth pangs, be able to tackle between one and two projects a year. The use of an outside consulting group working with a company group will reduce this time quite significantly, perhaps by as much as 50 per cent. An outside commercial consulting group will probably charge up to about $250 (U.S.) or £50 (U.K.) per man day for its services, the actual cost depending on the degree of experience and seniority of the men involved. The academic group will probably take more time to study industrial problems than will consulting firms but their fees will of course be rather less.

If you are considering a contract with an outside consulting firm we would strongly suggest cost-based rather than fixed-fee contracts. It is not possible to estimate accurately the cost of an OR job in advance. An experienced OR group will be able to estimate the upper and lower bounds for a job and such professional groups will make every attempt to stay within the limits involved.

A major part, perhaps three-quarters, of the time spent on an OR job is devoted to gathering and processing data. Hence the availability and quality of data is perhaps the most important factor in effecting the length of an OR study. The use of company personnel in collecting data has a double-edged advantage. First of all, they are far more likely to know where the data lie than is an outside group; and, secondly, using an outside group for collecting and processing data is more expensive than using internal company personnel for this particular phase of an OR task.

One of the principal by-products of an OR activity in a company is that it generally leads to a significantly improved data-collection system which reduces time required for future studies and which has many supplementary advantages for management.

OR in small businesses

The time and cost involved in OR seems to preclude its use by small firms. Most of the companies with internal OR groups have gross annual sales of over $30,000,000 in the U.S. and £5,000,000 (U.K.) What then can be done by a small firm which still wishes to use OR in its activities on a continuing basis? There are a number of alternatives.

1. The firm can retain one man who can be used in OR and other research activities as well. When he is used in OR he can be supplemented by personnel borrowed for the specific problem or by men recruited or hired from outside.

2. Most small firms, including even the very smallest, can afford to support a graduate student who is working in OR and who is willing to do his thesis on the company's problem. The student may not be industrially experienced but he will be under the supervision of competent men in his university. The universities which might be approached to give help on these lines are those which offer advanced degrees in OR. Such a student could be supported by amounts varying from £350 to £500 a year or $2,000 to $4,000 a year. A direct approach should be made to the universities concerned.

3. The small firm concerned might have access to a research association which works on behalf of the whole of its industry. This can be a most powerful way of carrying out OR. Any research association worth its salt will welcome the chance of being invited to develop OR for one of its member firms.

Physical facilities and equipment required by an OR team

Fortunately, the physical facilities required by an OR team are very modest. It obviously requires office space and it is a great help if you can do this on the basis of one man per office, or at most, two men per office. A small conference room will be useful if the offices are too small to hold all the men involved. In addition, to such obvious requirements as desks, bookcases, filing cabinets, the team will require:

1. One fully automatic desk calculator for about every five men, or preferably one to every three men if you can afford this.
2. Plenty of blackboard space so that problems may be worked out in a way in which it is easy for people to join. You should work on the basis of at least twenty square feet of blackboard per man.
3. Reference library of basic works and journals.

There are a number of specialist libraries available. In the U.K. the best is probably that at the Comrie Library, 23 Bedford Square, London, W.C.1. In the U.S.A., the universities offering advanced degrees have complete OR libraries. One must, however, be prepared to buy textbooks for your OR workers. They are, after all, trained and qualified scientists and their life blood is the literature of their subject. $500 or £100 should be enough to provide an adequate initial library and you should allow a further $200 or £50 a year for current journals and new books.

There is a delusion that electronic computers are a necessary requirement in OR. Nothing could be further from the truth. Access to computers is necessary and your team will occasionally need to rent computer time in service agencies or from other firms. Do, however, make sure that you keep your OR group separate from the computers. They can work closely together, but these are distinct activities and it is easy for one to become the slave of the other.

Companies which have used or are using OR

It is not possible to provide a complete list of such companies but you may find it interesting to see some of the principal users.

This list has been drawn up by our personal knowledge and also from the lists of full members of the Operations Research Society of America and the Operational Research Society of the United Kingdom.

UNITED STATES*	UNITED KINGDOM
Aircraft and Missiles	
Aerojet General	Boulton Paul Aircraft
Aerospace	Hawker Siddeley
American Power Jet	Royal Aircraft Establishment

* Including a few in Canada.

G

Aircraft and Missiles (cont.)

Bendix Aviation
Boeing
Chance Vought Aircraft
Convair
Douglas Aircraft
Fairchild Engine & Aircraft
Glenn L. Martin
Goodyear Aircraft
Hughes Aircraft
Lockheed Aircraft
McDonnell Aircraft
North American Aviation
Northrop
Republic Aviation
Sandia
Tempco Aircraft

Auto and Related

Cleveland Graphite Bronze
Cummins Engine
Ford Motor
General Motors
International Harvester
S.K.F. Industries
Timken Roller Bearing
Thompson Ramo Wooldridge
Vickers Hydraulics
Westinghouse Airbrake

Banking and Investment

Bank of America   Phillipps & Drew
Chase Manhattan Bank

Brewing and Liquor

Brown Forman Distillers   Distillers Coy.
Jos. Schlitz Brewery   Guinness
Schenley Distillers

Building Products and Equipment

A. O. Smith   —
General Dynamics
H. I. Thompson Fiber Glass
Johns-Mansville Products
Pittsburgh Plate Glass

UNITED STATES　　　　　UNITED KINGDOM

Building Products and Equipment (cont.)

Rheem Manufacturing
The Budd Coy.

Chemical

Atlas Chemical Industries	Albright & Wilson
Commercial Solvents	British Oxygen
Diamond Alkali	British Resin Products
Dow Chemical	W. J. Bush
Dupont	J. Crosfield
E. I. du Pont de Nemours	Distillers Coy.
Monsanto Chemical	Fisons
The Carborundum Co.	Imperial Chemical Industries
Union Carbide & Carbon	Laporte Industries
Velsicol Chemical	Shell Chemicals
	Unilever

Construction

—　　　　Cementation Coy.

Communications

American District Telegraph　　　General Post Office
American Tel. & Tel.
Bell Telephone Laboratories
International Electric
I.T. & T.
Mountain States Tel. & Tel.
Western Electric

Electrical, Electronic and Computer

American Bosch Arma	Associated Electrical Industries
Bendix	Cossors
Burroughs	Decca
Conductron	E.M.I.
Crossley Avco	English Electric
General Electric	General Electric Company
General Precision	International Computers and
General Radio	Tabulators
I.B.M.	Mullard
Litton Industries	Phillips
Lockheed Electronics	
Minneapolis-Honeywell	
Motorola	
National Cash Register	
Philco	

UNITED STATES   UNITED KINGDOM

Electrical, Electronic and Computer (cont)

R.C.A.
Ramo-Wooldridge
Raytheon
Royal Precision
Sperry-Rand
Sylvania Electric Products
Telecomputing
Texas Instrument
Westinghouse Electric
Whirlpool

Industrial Equipment

American Machine and Foundry	British Ropes
Barber-Coleman	Hepworth & Grandage
Cleveland Pneumatic Ind.	National Institute of Agricultural
Hughes Tool	Engineering
Warner Swasey	R. H. Neal
	Sigmund Pumps

Insurance

Acacia Mutual Life Ins.   —
Allstate Insurance
Bankers Life & Casualty
British Pacific Life Ins.
Consolidated American Life Insurance
Equitable Life Assurance
Metropolitan Life Insurance
New York Life Insurance
Prudential Insurance
West Coast Life Insurance

Merchandizing

A.M.C. Stores	John Lewis
Bamburger's	Littlewoods
Sears, Roebuck	Saxone
Stix, Baer, & Fuller	Lilley & Skinner

Metals

Aluminium Co. of America	British Aluminium
Continental Can	British Iron & Steel Research
Inland Steel	Association
Henry J. Kaiser	Colvilles
Johns & Laughlin Steel	Gillette
Mallory-Sharon Titanium	Guest Keen and Nettlefolds

UNITED STATES	UNITED KINGDOM

Metals (cont.)

Republic Steel	Steel Company of Wales
U.S. Steel	Richard Thomas & Baldwins
Youngstown Sheet & Tube	Tube Investments
	United Steel Company

Mining

Cleveland Cliffs	British Coal Utilization Research
International Minerals and Chemicals	Association
M. A. Hanna	National Coal Board
Minnesota Mining & Mfg.	Rio Tinto

Packaged Goods

Armour	Batchelors Foods
General Foods	Cadbury
General Mills	Petfoods
Hunt Food & Industries	Unilever
M & M Candies	
Cahu Sugar	
Proctor & Gamble	

Paper

Canadian International Paper	A. E. Reed
Champion Paper & Fiber	Wiggins Teape
Kimberly-Clark	
Scott Paper	
West Virginia Pub. & Paper	

Petroleum

Atlantic Refining	British Petroleum
British American Oil	Esso
City Service Oil	Shell International
Ethyl	Shell Mex-B.P.
Esso Standard	
Gulf Oil	
Imperial Oil	
Jenney Mfg.	
Ohio Oil	
Phillips Petroleum	
Pure Oil	
Richfield Oil	
Shell Development	
Shell Oil	
Socony Mobil Oil	
Standard Oil of California	

UNITED STATES	UNITED KINGDOM
Petroleum (cont.)	
Standard Oil (Indiana)	
Standard Oil (Ohio)	
Sun Oil	
Union Oil	
Pharmaceuticals	
Abbot Laboratories	—
Charles Pfizer	
Eli Lilly	
Smith, Kline & French	
Squibb	
Photography	
Eastman Kodak	Ilford
	Kodak
Printing and Publishing	
American Greetings	Macmillan
Curtis Publishing	Odhams Press
Mergenthaler Linotype	Whitefriars Press
World Publishing	
Xerox	
Public Surveys	
—	Gallup Polls
	Television Audience Measurement
Restaurants	
—	J. Lyons
Rubber	
General Tire and Rubber	—
U.S. Rubber	
Shoe Manufacture	
—	British Boot, Shoe & Allied Trades Research Assoc.
Textiles	
Celanese	British Celanese
Hanes Hosiery Mills	British Nylon Spinners
Rayco Auto Seat Covers	Courtaulds
	Shirley Institute

UNITED STATES	UNITED KINGDOM

Tobacco

Reynolds Tobacco	Tobacco Manufacturers Standing Committee

Transport

American Airlines	British European Airways
Canadian National Railways	British Overseas Airways Corp.
Chesapeake & Ohio R.R.	British Transport Commission
Chicago & North Western Railway Co.	London Transport Executive
Greyhound	
Illinois Central Railroad	
Matson Navigation	
Railway Express Agency	
Southern Pacific Railroad	
Trans Canada Airlines	
United Airlines	

Utilities

Cleveland Electric Illuminating	Central Electricity Generating Board
Hydro Electric Power Comm. of Ontario	United Kingdom Atomic Energy Authority

Wood Products

—	Timber Development Assoc.

Do OR projects ever fail?

The last thing we wish to leave with the reader is the thought that OR is a universal remedy for all management's ailments. Nothing could be further from the truth. OR can fail and has failed. Fortunately, it does not happen very often and when it has happened there are assignable reasons for this occurring. We have never been involved in a case where the solution just did not work. Frequently, of course, a solution does not work exactly as predicted, but the deviation is seldom serious and adjustments can usually be made to correct for minor oversights.

The most common type of failure occurs when results are not accepted and hence are not implemented. In some cases implementation is only partial and in other cases there has been an apparent glib acceptance of the results which is followed by a period of masterly inactivity. The principal reasons for failure and hence the principal reasons for not obtaining complete implementation seem to fall into the following categories.

1. The company is reorganized during the study so that the managers responsible for the study are replaced.

In situations of this type the new manager is usually preoccupied with his new responsibilities and shows no interest in becoming involved in what he considers to be the fine points of his operation. In some such instances, he eventually becomes interested in the study, after he is thoroughly 'broken-in'. In other cases he never does become interested, often because he did not initiate the study and he wants to disassociate himself from his predecessor (particularly an unsuccessful predecessor) in every way he can.

We know of no effective way of avoiding this difficulty. It does help to have the 'number two man' involved as well as 'number one' because the second man may take the place of the first, or he may continue in his post when his boss is replaced, and thus provide some continuity and access to the new manager.

2. Lack of involvement of a high enough level of management either to assure access to all the needed data or to enforce necessary interdepartmental cooperation.

Some managers are inclined to shield their bosses from researchers and hence refuse to give their OR men access to higher authorities. We have had several cases in which the project could not be completed because necessary contacts at higher levels could not be made. For this reason, we find it desirable to involve at least one level of management higher than that which appears to be required initially in any study. Preferably, top level management should be kept informed and be invited to attend reviews of the research. Such breakdowns are rare where top management has been involved along the way.

3. Attempts by individuals to use the research to further some personal, rather than the organization's, objective.

In some cases before initiating the research a manager has taken a position as to what the solution would be and he intends the research to prove himself correct. If the research begins to indicate that he was wrong he may find it difficult to save face, and sometimes prefers to suppress the research findings or discredit them on irrational grounds.

4. Economic pressures that lead to a reduction of expenses including those for research.

Little need be said about this point except to note that OR may be able to show either how to 'retrench' in the least costly way or what steps to take to change the situation.

In general we think that if the following principles are followed, failure to implement results will become less frequent:

1. The OR team should never report to anyone lower than the authority capable of controlling all the functions involved in the study. It is not enough to have managers of each of the relevant functions represented in a reviewing group; the group should contain a manager of sufficiently high level to assure cooperation between the functions represented in the group.

2. Reports to the responsible authorities should be made by the researchers themselves, not through intermediaries. This avoids the intrusion of ulterior motives and misrepresentation of findings.

3. The cost of the research should be borne by those for whom it is conducted. Managers tend to have little respect for what they get for nothing. They generally suspect, and with some justification, the motives lying behind free offerings. Management's sense of responsibility for an activity tends to be directly proportionate to the amount it must pay for that activity.

4. Finally, it must be confessed that in many cases the results of a project are reported and presented in a slipshod fashion. It is simply no use for a team to be invited to carry out a study, to do their study, to analyze the results and then to write up a report and slip it through the letter box of the manager concerned. To carry out such a course is to invite disaster. Equally, an invitation to disaster occurs when a team, without prior consultation, writes up its report and sends it out to all the members of a committee. People should not receive an OR report cold. The ways to present the reports of a study are first of all to have frequent meetings with the management concerned throughout the progress of a study, and then when the results are completed and the investigation is finished, to have an informal meeting at which all the tables and graphs are presented pictorially by means of large pictures on pieces of paper, so that there may be a frank and informal discussion of the way in which the team is thinking and the conclusions which they are tentatively reaching. The

report, when it is written, should be a document agreed upon by all the people who are going to receive it. In this way, objections can be anticipated and dealt with and the whole work is terminated in a smoother fashion.

Now that types of failures have been considered something should be also said about unplanned-for-success; that is, useful by-products of OR of which there seem to be two important types. First, by their systematic questioning of managers responsible for an activity, and by the example of their analytic and objective approach to problems, OR men generally produce increased efforts by managers to be thorough and more analytical in the decisions they make. In general, the presence of OR tends to upgrade the quality of decision making by others in the organization. Secondly, in the course of OR simple things are often uncovered which yield an immediate and significant payoff.

Will OR take over management?

This is a blunt question and demands a blunt answer. The answer is quite simple—No. Management, in fact, will take over OR. Let us explain what we mean by this.

The skills and knowledge required of managers have expanded considerably in this century. Today, as contrasted with fifty years ago, some specialized college preparation is generally expected of those who aspire to management. Managers have had to learn the complexities of each phase of business, and they have had to become expert in at least one of these. There is no reason to expect that the requirement to learn new things will disappear.

As OR accumulates more experience it will develop the ability to solve certain types of problems in a routine way. These will be relegated to what might eventually be called 'Operational Engineering'. Here the techniques and general principles which have been found by OR will be applied without research. It can be expected that, in the future, management education will require knowledge of these techniques and principles and how and where to apply them.

There are strong indications of this already. Courses in OR are already wide-spread in business schools. Stimulated by the recent reports on management education by the Ford and Carnegie Foundations, most business schools are adding considerable work in quantitative methods. Hence, the generation of managers now being produced are capable of some use of OR. The next generation will be capable of considerably more. There is little doubt that management is gradually becoming an applied science. This is not to say that 'art' is being eliminated from management; one has only to look at science in which art has never been completely eliminated.

As operational engineering emerges and managers become capable of practicing it, OR workers will move on to problems of even greater complexity than those with which they deal today. We can look forward to the conversion of the courtship of management and science into a lasting marriage through which more effective control of more complex organizations can be assured.

Conclusion

In all our experience of OR we have seen that the carrying out of OR studies and their successful completion does not remove from the manager the task of decision-making but rather it requires of him that he makes rather different kinds of decision. The OR worker is to the manager what the telescope is to the astronomer and the microscope to the biologist. Astronomers, before they had telescopes, had to work in a very difficult fashion and had to develop their subject in a very halting fashion. The provision of the telescope did not mean that we no longer required astronomers but rather that it gave them an extra insight into their particular subject and hence led them into much more difficult areas. The simple problems, such as the logging of the movements of the planet and of the occurrence of eclipses were now past and they were led into the highly sophisticated problems of the Newtonian and the Einsteinian approaches to gravitation. Equally, management in a company which has a highly successful OR group carrying out studies in which the conclusions are taken note of and acted on will find that it is called upon to study different problems, to take different decisions which are themselves much more important, and intellectually much more difficult, than the original problems with which they were dealing on a day-to-day basis. We would say to the managers of industry that so far as their own selfish ends are concerned, so far as the delight they can take and the satisfaction they can achieve in their day-to-day activities are concerned, that this is the chief and most compelling reason for them doing OR. We believe that their lives and their jobs will become infinitely more interesting if they have an OR group reporting to them.

Let us finally end with a declaration of our faith with the task of the OR worker. It can be said with justification that his task is to advise executives and managers but not to take the decisions himself. The ultimate responsibility for the decisions still rests with the executive or the manager. With this we agree, provided that certain conditions are met by the OR worker. First of all, he must feel fully committed to the decision to which he has come. He must be prepared, if invited to do so by the executive concerned, to say what decision he would undertake if he were sitting in the manager's chair. It is not sufficient for an OR worker to go to a manager and say: 'On the basis of the study I have carried out, the alternative decisions you can make are this, this and this, and what is likely to happen if you undertake particular courses of action are this, this and this.' If the manager then says to him: 'Well, on the basis of my empirical knowledge, I really feel that I will still carry out a particular course of action which either is not considered in your model or alternatively looks a very stupid course of action in your model,' then it is clear that the OR work itself has been quite useless. The OR worker must be able to reach out into the background of experience of the manager concerned and to bring it forward and to develop into his models the relevant factors from this experience. To offer advice without accepting responsibility for it is to claim power without responsibility. The privilege of the OR worker is not to advise and retreat but to advise and commit. With every job which the OR worker does he must at the conclusion of the job place his own reputation on the table with his report. He must be willing to be judged by the manager in exactly the same way that the manager has to be judged, namely, on the basis of the performance of his recommendations when they are put into operation.

5 Further Reading

WE HOPE that by now you will feel that you have some understanding of OR. We have purposely kept this book short, since there is nothing so depressing as introductions of inordinate length. If we have stimulated your appetite this far, it is possible that you will be moved to introduce OR to others. Alternatively and additionally, you may feel that you want to read further and to browse through the literature. In this last chapter we shall try to take you on a very brief guided tour of OR publications, so that you can select the books and papers which meet your particular needs.

There are a few popular accounts of operational research which we recommend. Two of these are written from the business man's standpoint and the other to meet the requirements of the scientist who wishes to know something about this new field. For the business man we would recommend two articles by Herbert Solow, published in *Fortune* magazine, in April 1951, and in February 1956. For those in the human sciences we suggest Robert Dorfman, 'Operations Research', *American Economic Review*, pp. 575–623 (1960).

For the manager who wants to know something of the techniques of operational research there is a highly simplified and highly selective account in *A Guide to Operational Research* by Eric Duckworth (Methuen, London, 1962). An alternative account of techniques in a rather wider area of application is a well-written book by B. T. Houlden, *Some Techniques of Operational Research* (English Universities Press, London, 1961). If you want to flex your mathematical muscles, then try *Operations Research— Methods and Problems* by M. W. Sasieni, A. Yaspan and L. Friedman (Wiley, New York, 1959).

Case study material is a very important way of understanding the subject and there are a number of books which are worth reading. These include *Operations Research for Management* by

McCloskey and Trefethen, Volume I, and by McCloskey and Dissinger, Volume II (Johns Hopkins Press, Baltimore, 1954 and 1956). Wide ranging surveys of case studies and of theoretical developments are given in *The Proceedings of the First International Conference on Operational Research* (English Universities Press, London, 1958), and *The Proceedings of the Second International Conference on Operational Research* (English Universities Press, London, 1961). A number of case studies are presented in *Operations Research* and in the *Operational Research Quarterly*. On reading these journals, you may have the impression that OR consists of a collection of slick mathematical tricks. This is an entirely false impression which arises because in many cases, owing to industrial secrecy, OR workers are unable to publish full case studies. When you take away the data and the description of the organization involved, it is inevitable that one is left with a collection of mathematics. Hence the biased appearance of the literature is a reflection of the conditions under which much OR is carried out, rather than of the actual subject matter.

There are a number of books which give general accounts of the theory of OR. Among these, we recommend:

Introduction to Operations Research by C. W. Churchman, R. L. Ackoff and E. L. Arnoff (Wiley, New York, 1957)

Operational Research in Management by R. T. Eddison, K. Pennycuick and B. H. P. Rivett (English Universities Press, London, 1961)

Executive Decisions and Operations Research by D. W. Miller and M. K. Starr (Prentice Hall, New Jersey, 1960)

The Analysis of Industrial Operations by E. H. Bowman and R. B. Fetter (Irwin, Illinois, 1959)

These four references all deal with the theory and practice of OR and cover a wide range of the subject. A useful series, which covers current progress and developments, is one under the heading *Progress in Operations Research* published by Wiley, New York. The first volume by R. L. Ackoff was issued in 1961 and its successor, covering 1962, is now in preparation.

There are a number of publications which cover special areas of the application of OR. These are all reports of proceedings of conferences held at the Case Institute of Technology, Cleveland, and are all published by Case Institute. They are:

Proceedings of the Conference on Operations Research in Marketing, 1953

Proceedings of the Conference on Operations Research in Production and Inventory Control, 1954

Proceedings of the Conference on Operations Research, Computers and Management Decisions, 1957

Proceedings of the Conference on Applications of Operations Research to Research and Development (to be published by Wiley, New York)

In addition, there is an admirable non-technical survey, *Production Planning and Inventory Control* by J. Magee (McGraw-Hill, New York, 1958)

There remain two areas which bracket the above list. At this stage of the development of the subject, it is still of interest to read the first textbook in OR which also includes some of the history of the subject. This is *Methods of Operations Research* by P. M. Morse and G. E. Kimball (The Technology Press of Massachusetts Institute of Technology and John Wiley and Sons, New York, first edition revised, 1951). Finally, in these days when operational research is moving into problems of government and of large-scale planning, one of the best accounts of what is implied in this approach is contained in the early chapters of *A Computable Model of Economic Growth* by R. Stone and A. Brown (Chapman and Hall, London, 1962).

These, then, are the suggestions we make for further reading. We cannot claim that every one of these books will dazzle you with sparkling style and narrative display. Nevertheless, they present a spectrum ranging from the popular non-technical account through to the sophisticated mathematical techniques. However, it still remains true that the best way of learning what operations research is about is to talk with OR workers, to find out from them the problems on which they are engaged and to get from them something of the flavour of this science.

We hope you will find it to your taste.

References

Ackoff, R. L., 'Towards a Behavioral Theory of Communications', *Management Science*, 4 (1958), 218–234; (ed), *Progress in Operations Research*, Vol. I. John Wiley and Sons, New York, 1961.

Arnoff, E. K. and Sengupta, S. A., 'Mathematical Programming', in Ackoff (1961), 105–210.

Arrow, K. J., Karlin, S. and Scarf, H., *Studies in the Mathematical Theory of Inventory and Production*. Stanford University Press, Stanford, California, 1958.

Cherry, Colin, *On Human Communication*. John Wiley and Sons, New York, 1957.

Churchman, C. W., Ackoff, R. L. and Arnoff, E. L., *Introduction to Operations Research*, John Wiley and Sons, New York, 1957.

Cohen, K. J. and Rhenman, Eric, 'The Role of Management Games in Education and Research', *Management Science*, 7 (1961), 131–166.

Cox, D. R. and Smith, W. L., *Queues*. Methuen, London, 1961.

Crowther, J. G. and Whiddington, R., *Science at War*, Her Majesty's Stationery Office, London, 1947.

Dean, B. V., 'Replacement Theory', in Ackoff (1961), 327–362.

Dreyfus, Stuart, 'Dynamic Programming', in Ackoff (1961), 211–242.

Eddison, R. T. and Owen, D. G., 'Discharging Iron Ore', *Operational Research Quarterly* (September 1953).

Eddison, R. T., Pennycuick, K. P. and Rivett, B. H. P. 'Operational Research in Management', English Universities Press, 1961.

Haire, Mason (ed), *Modern Organization Theory*. John Wiley and Sons, New York, 1959.

Hanssmann, Fred, 'A Survey of Inventory Theory from the Operations Research Viewpoint'', in Ackoff (1961), 35–64.

Houlden, B. T., *Some Techniques of Operational Research*, English Universities Press, 1961.

Kelley, J. E., Jr., 'Critical-Path Planning and Scheduling: Mathematical Basis', *Operations Research*, 9 (1961), 296–320.

Magee, J. F., *Production Planning and Inventory Control*. McGraw-Hill, New York, 1958.

Malcolm, D. G., Roseboom, J. H., Clark, C. E. and Fazar, W., 'Applications of a Technique for Research and Development Evaluation', *Operations Research*, 7 (1959), 646–669.

Morse, P. M., *Queues, Inventories and Maintenance*. John Wiley and Sons, New York, 1958.

H

Shannon, C. E. and Weaver, W., *The Mathematical Theory of Communication*. University of Illinois Press, Urbana, Illinois, 1949.

Sisson, R. L., "Sequencing Theory", in Ackoff (1961), 293–326.

Syski, R., *Introduction to Congestion Theory in Telephone Systems*. Oliver and Boyd, Edinburgh, 1960.

Williams, J. D., *The Compleat Strategyst*. McGraw-Hill, New York, 1954.

Index